INTRODUCING
ISSUES WITH
OPPOSING
VIEWPOINTS®

Terrorism

Lauri S. Friedman, *Book Editor*

GREENHAVEN PRESS
A part of Gale, Cengage Learning

GALE
CENGAGE Learning™

Detroit • New York • San Francisco • New Haven, Conn • Waterville, Maine • London

Christine Nasso, *Publisher*
Elizabeth Des Chenes, *Managing Editor*

For more information, contact:
Greenhaven Press
27500 Drake Rd.
Farmington Hills, MI 48331-3535
Or you can visit our Internet site at gale.cengage.com

Articles in Greenhaven Press anthologies are often edited for length to meet page requirements. In addition, original titles of these works are changed to clearly present the main thesis and to explicitly indicate the author's opinion. Every effort is made to ensure that Greenhaven Press accurately reflects the original intent of the authors. Every effort has been made to trace the owners of copyrighted material.

LIBRARY OF CONGRESS CATALOGING-IN-PUBLICATION DATA

Terrorism / Lauri S. Friedman, book editor.
   p. cm. -- (Introducing issues with opposing viewpoints)
 Includes bibliographical references and index.
 ISBN 978-0-7377-4944-1 (hbk.)
 1. Terrorism--Juvenile literature. 2. Terrorism--Prevention--Juvenile literature. I.
Friedman, Lauri S.
   HV6431.T45763 2010
   363.325--dc22
                                                                  2010023161

Printed in the United States of America
1 2 3 4 5 6 7 14 13 12 11 10

Contents

Foreword

I ndulging in a wide spectrum of ideas, beliefs, and perspectives is a critical cornerstone of democracy. After all, it is often debates over differences of opinion, such as whether to legalize abortion, how to treat prisoners, or when to enact the death penalty, that shape our society and drive it forward. Such diversity of thought is frequently regarded as the hallmark of a healthy and civilized culture. As the Reverend Clifford Schutjer of the First Congregational Church in Mansfield, Ohio, declared in a 2001 sermon, "Surrounding oneself with only like-minded people, restricting what we listen to or read only to what we find agreeable is irresponsible. Refusing to entertain doubts once we make up our minds is a subtle but deadly form of arrogance." With this advice in mind, Introducing Issues with Opposing Viewpoints books aim to open readers' minds to the critically divergent views that comprise our world's most important debates.

Introducing Issues with Opposing Viewpoints simplifies for students the enormous and often overwhelming mass of material now available via print and electronic media. Collected in every volume is an array of opinions that captures the essence of a particular controversy or topic. Introducing Issues with Opposing Viewpoints books embody the spirit of nineteenth-century journalist Charles A. Dana's axiom: "Fight for your opinions, but do not believe that they contain the whole truth, or the only truth." Absorbing such contrasting opinions teaches students to analyze the strength of an argument and compare it to its opposition. From this process readers can inform and strengthen their own opinions, or be exposed to new information that will change their minds. Introducing Issues with Opposing Viewpoints is a mosaic of different voices. The authors are statesmen, pundits, academics, journalists, corporations, and ordinary people who have felt compelled to share their experiences and ideas in a public forum. Their words have been collected from newspapers, journals, books, speeches, interviews, and the Internet, the fastest growing body of opinionated material in the world.

Introducing Issues with Opposing Viewpoints shares many of the well-known features of its critically acclaimed parent series, Opposing Viewpoints. The articles are presented in a pro/con format, allowing readers to absorb divergent perspectives side by side. Active reading questions preface each viewpoint, requiring the student to approach the material thoughtfully and carefully. Useful charts, graphs, and cartoons supplement each article. A thorough introduction provides readers with crucial background on an issue. An annotated bibliography points the reader toward articles, books, and Web sites that contain additional information on the topic. An appendix of organizations to contact contains a wide variety of charities, nonprofit organizations, political groups, and private enterprises that each hold a position on the issue at hand. Finally, a comprehensive index allows readers to locate content quickly and efficiently.

Introducing Issues with Opposing Viewpoints is also significantly different from Opposing Viewpoints. As the series title implies, its presentation will help introduce students to the concept of opposing viewpoints and learn to use this material to aid in critical writing and debate. The series' four-color, accessible format makes the books attractive and inviting to readers of all levels. In addition, each viewpoint has been carefully edited to maximize a reader's understanding of the content. Short but thorough viewpoints capture the essence of an argument. A substantial, thought-provoking essay question placed at the end of each viewpoint asks the student to further investigate the issues raised in the viewpoint, compare and contrast two authors' arguments, or consider how one might go about forming an opinion on the topic at hand. Each viewpoint contains sidebars that include at-a-glance information and handy statistics. A Facts About section located in the back of the book further supplies students with relevant facts and figures.

Following in the tradition of the Opposing Viewpoints series, Greenhaven Press continues to provide readers with invaluable exposure to the controversial issues that shape our world. As John Stuart Mill once wrote: "The only way in which a human being can make some approach to knowing the whole of a subject is by hearing what can be said about it by persons of every variety of opinion and studying all modes in which it can be looked at by every character of mind. No wise man ever acquired his wisdom in any mode but this." It is to this principle that Introducing Issues with Opposing Viewpoints books are dedicated.

Introduction

A decade into the war on terror, law enforcement authorities have yet to identify a set of defining qualities or characteristics that are common to all terrorists. Terrorists have come from more than a dozen countries, practice every religion, and exhibit no clear psychological pattern. Terrorists have been both men and women, single and married, educated and unskilled, children and elderly. People have committed terrorist acts for a vast array of reasons: to express political grievances, to secure themselves a homeland, to drive out a foreign invader, and to intimidate a population into acquiescing to their demands. In other words, there *is* no exact terrorist profile, and the notion of terrorists as being young, male, poor, and religious is increasingly being proved inaccurate. As security expert Henry Morgenstern puts it, "The idea that the suicide terrorist act is the endeavor of a deranged individual, who is a young male and a fundamentalist fanatic, is totally wrong. The potential suicide terrorist may actually come from different backgrounds, different age groups, be male or female, educated or uneducated, an upstanding citizen or a deviant."[1]

Though it has long been thought that terrorists are overwhelmingly poor and disenfranchised, evidence from the world's highest-profile terrorist plots indicates otherwise. Certainly some terrorists have come from impoverished communities and committed their terrible crimes as a response to suffering from hopelessness and despair. Yet increasing evidence reveals that many of the world's terrorists have come from middle-class, upper-middle-class, and even wealthy families. These people have studied in some of the most elite universities and lived in some of the world's most glamorous cities, indulging in a lifestyle of wealth and privilege while they do so. In fact, the phenomenon of the "privileged terrorist" is one that increasingly baffles and fascinates U.S. terrorism experts.

That terrorists often hail from backgrounds of privilege and class is well documented. Indeed, the world's most notorious terrorist—al Qaeda leader Osama bin Laden—is one of the world's wealthiest families. Bin Laden is not merely rich: He is a billionaire. Some of his closest associates are also members of the upper class.

Osama bin Laden comes from a background of wealth, privilege, and class.

For example, Ayman al-Zawahiri, his top deputy, is a doctor from a wealthy Egyptian family; Mohamed Atta, the al Qaeda operative who led the September 11 attacks, was a highly educated Egyptian from a wealthy family of lawyers, doctors, traders, and professors. Fifteen of the September 11 hijackers came from Saudi Arabia, one of the world's wealthiest nations.

Other terrorists have come from similarly privileged backgrounds. Columnist Jamie Weinstein reports that one of the bombers responsible for the July 7, 2005, attack on the London public transit system—in which fifty-six people were killed—left behind an estate worth more than $150,000. Similarly privileged is Umar Farouk Abdulmutallab, a Nigerian-born al Qaeda operative who attempted to blow up a Northwest Airlines flight from Amsterdam to Detroit on December 25, 2009, by hiding explosives in his underwear. Despite his radical leanings, Abdulmutallab lived a particularly elite life. He studied for three years at a choice college in London, where he lived in a fancy apartment valued at 2 million British pounds (about $4 million). His father is the former economics minister of Nigeria and holds a seat on the board of several of Nigeria's biggest firms. As author Salil Tripathi puts it, these terrorists "didn't lack material wealth; they lacked the sensitivity to value human life."[2]

Several studies have cast further doubt on the poverty-terrorism connection. A 2003 study by Rand economist Claude Berrebi, for example, found that only 13 percent of Palestinian suicide bombers come from impoverished families. In fact, Berrebi's fifteen-year study of Palestinian terrorists revealed they have been, on average, better educated and more affluent than the Palestinian Arab population as a whole. A 2005 study of Arab insurgents in Iraq by Reuven Paz came to a similar conclusion, finding that many of those who have been killed fighting came from middle-class or wealthy families.

Perhaps the clearest indicator that poverty is an unlikely motivator of terrorism is that millions of people live in poverty around the world, yet very few of them take up terrorism. Indeed, terrorists make up a minuscule percentage of the world's inhabitants; the poor, on the other hand, make up around 20 percent of the global population. The poor do not routinely explode buildings or buses to express their discontent. If they did so, the number of terrorist attacks would be much higher than the roughly eleven thousand that the National Counterterrorism Center says occur each year. "While politicians and even many academics continue to propound the supposed connection between poverty and terrorism, the actual evidence doesn't support this convenient link," writes Weinstein. "If there was such a strong connection, the phrase 'Cambodian suicide bomber' would be quite familiar instead of unheard of."[3]

Who commits acts of terrorism and how they can be prevented is just one of the issues explored in *Introducing Issues with Opposing Viewpoints: Terrorism*. Other problems and questions—such as how serious is the threat from terrorism, whether terrorists are likely to commit an attack using a weapon of mass destruction, and whether captured terrorists should be tortured or given the death penalty—are explored in pro/con article pairs by passionate, expert voices on the topic. Guided reading questions and essay prompts lead readers to form their own opinions on this enduring issue.

Notes

1. Henry Morgenstern, "Suicide Terror: Is Law Enforcement Ready?" *Law Enforcement Technology*, September 2006, p. 32.
2. Salil Tripathi, "Debunking the Poverty-Terrorism Myth," *Asian Wall Street Journal*, February 23, 2005.
3. Jamie Weinstein, "Most Terrorists Are Privileged Terrorists," *Washington Examiner*, January 3, 2010. www.washingtonexaminer.com/opinion/columns/OpEd-Contributor/Jamie-Weinstein-Most-terrorists-are-privileged-terrorists-80537247.html.

Chapter 1

How Serious Is the Terrorist Threat?

The May 2010 bombing attempt
of Times Square in New York City
reminded Americans that terrorists still
seek to do them harm.

Terrorists Pose a Serious Threat to the United States

Diane Dimond

"America's fight against terrorism is far from over. The battlefield is worldwide."

In the following viewpoint Diane Dimond argues that the terrorist threat to America continues to be real and dangerous. She offers several examples in which terrorists plotted to attack major targets in large American cities but were apprehended by authorities before they had the chance to do any damage. According to Dimond, these are just a few examples of the many people who are out there plotting attacks against the United States. Dimond says America's law enforcement officials are constantly investigating terrorist tips and apprehending people who plot to hurt innocent Americans and their property. She concludes there are many would-be terrorists who wish to hurt Americans, and this is why, in her opinion, the American government needs to take the war on terror more seriously.

Dimond is a television journalist best known for her work as a correspondent on the shows *Hard Copy*, *Extra*, and *Entertainment Tonight*.

AS YOU READ, CONSIDER THE FOLLOWING QUESTIONS:
  1. What did Najibullah Zazi plan to do, according to Dimond?
  2. Who is Michael Finton, and how does the author factor him into her argument?
  3. According to Dimond, on what charges did New York authorities arrest three U.S. citizens and a Haitian man in May 2009?

Crime happens when we least expect it. Criminal activity festers in places we can't imagine and in the minds of those we least expect. We should not be surprised when it is discovered.

The recent [2009] arrest of three seemingly low-key, nondescript men on charges of lying to federal agents about a plot to blow up American targets sounds like the stuff Hollywood makes movies about. But these arrests were all too real and should go to remind us that America's fight against terrorism is far from over. The battlefield is worldwide.

Authorities Prevent Disaster

These most recent suspects, all foreign-born Muslims, include a 24-year-old Denver airport shuttle driver, his father and an alleged accomplice in New York. They have not, of course, been found guilty of anything. But their case seems destined to go to trial.

Before he stopped talking to the FBI, the suspected ring-leader, 24-year-old Najibullah Zazi, a native of Afghanistan, allegedly told agents he received al-Qaeda [an Islamist terrorist group] weapons training in Pakistan last year. An FBI document claims Zazi's laptop computer contained a recipe for bomb-making and information about important New York area targets like transportation hubs and sports and entertainment venues.

They tied Zazi's recent trip to New York (ominously on September 10, the day before the nation marked the 9-11 anniversary) to his fingerprints on bomb-making ingredients found in apartments he visited in Queens. Media reports and FBI documents mentioned suspicions that Zazi planned to place bombs in rented vans or backpacks. Authorities felt the plot had developed to include at least three separate teams of four men each preparing to carry out various U.S. attacks.

Countless Terrorists Have Been Stopped

The roundup of Zazi and his cohorts did not happen in a vacuum. Every day in this country—as far removed as we are from the day the towers fell, the Pentagon was struck and the jetliner crashed into the ground in rural Pennsylvania—special government agents are actively pursuing leads to thwart more terror attacks on American soil.

So far they've done a hell of a job. Operatives with the FBI, CIA, Homeland Security, your state and local police and other agencies know things about plots against our country that would curl your hair. They invisibly investigate countless cases we will never hear about, many times acting on tips from observant citizens.

Terrorists Are Plotting Among Us

[In September 2009] in Illinois an American ex-con who had converted to Islam in prison was arrested on charges he tried to blow up the federal building in Springfield. Michael Finton, also known as Talib Islam, was unknowingly working with local and federal law enforcement agents as he chose his target. He faces life in prison.

A day later in Dallas a Jordanian citizen was charged with trying to blow up a 60-story building with what he thought was an active car bomb. Actually, an FBI undercover agent posing as a fellow terrorist led 19-year-old Hosam Maher Husein Smadi to think he had genuine explosives. The suspect reportedly idolized [terrorist] Osama bin Laden.

In May [2009] New York authorities, along with the FBI arrested three U.S. citizens and a Haitian man on charges that they planned to bomb multiple synagogues in the Bronx and shoot down airplanes using surface-to-air missiles. In a meeting with a government informant one of the suspects revealed his parents lived in Afghanistan and he was angry about the U.S. war there. He said he had an interest in "doing something to America."

FAST FACT

According to the Heritage Foundation, at least thirty planned terrorist attacks have been foiled since the September 11, 2001, attacks. In 2009 alone, at least six plots were foiled.

Najibullah Zazi, center, is escorted by U.S. marshals upon his arrival in New York after being arrested for a plot to bomb the New York subway system on February 22, 2010.

All this talk about suspected terror plots in New York, Dallas and Springfield, Illinois might seem very far removed from where you live. But as we were all reminded on September 11, 2001 terrorism that touches one American city touches us all.

Americans Think Another Attack Is Likely

Polls show the majority of Americans think there will be another terrorist attack in the United States within a few months, and most feel the United States government should be doing more to protect them.

Question: "How likely do you think it is that there will be another terrorist attack in the United States within the next few months: very likely, somewhat likely, not very likely, or not at all likely?"

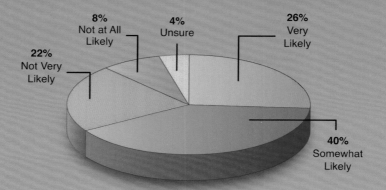

8%
Not at All
Likely

4%
Unsure

26%
Very
Likely

22%
Not Very
Likely

40%
Somewhat
Likely

Question: "Do you think U.S. intelligence agencies are doing all they could reasonably be expected to do to monitor the actions of suspected terrorists, or could they be doing more?"

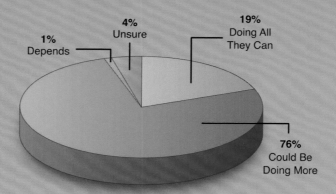

1%
Depends

4%
Unsure

19%
Doing All
They Can

76%
Could Be
Doing More

Taken from: CBS News poll, January 6–10, 2010.

America's Leaders Must Work Together

All these years after that awful day our leaders are still trying to figure out how to stop the terror at its source—those al-Qaeda sponsored training centers which pockmark the landscape in faraway places like Afghanistan and Pakistan. We've spent billions yet they survive. Why is that—are they smarter than us or do we lack conviction and a definitive plan for their eradication? I'll go with the latter. Our leaders cannot seem to get it together to stop this monster of all crimes.

Generals on the front line say they need another 30 thousand troops to mortally cripple al-Qaeda and bring some sort of democracy to the region. President [Barack Obama] has said he's prepared to allocate about 17 thousand more soldiers although he's now considering some alternatives too. Many members of Congress seem focused only on blaming the past for the quagmire and offer no suggestions on going forward, others on Capitol Hill support pulling out of the region right now, abandoning the mission altogether.

Democrats vs. Republicans, military leaders vs. civilian experts, soldier warriors vs. pacifists. America is strong enough and smart enough to figure it out. All we need is the right leadership.

So after an eight year war when do we begin to demand that?

EVALUATING THE AUTHORS' ARGUMENTS:

Dimond gives several examples of the ways in which the U.S. government has thwarted terrorist attacks to argue that the war on terror needs to be supported and even expanded. How do you think Philip Giraldi, author of the following viewpoint, would respond to this suggestion? After reading both viewpoints, with which author do you ultimately agree? List at least two pieces of evidence that swayed you.

The Threat Posed by Terrorists Has Been Exaggerated

Philip Giraldi

"The threat from terrorism has been greatly exaggerated for political reasons to create a sense of fear."

Terrorists do not pose a serious threat to the United States argues Philip Giraldi in the following viewpoint. He argues that many of the nations designated by the State Department as sponsors of terrorism pose no real threat to the United States. Some of the nations on the list have not been involved in terrorism in decades; others support political groups the United States simply does not like. Giraldi says even al Qaeda no longer poses a serious threat to the United States. He suggests that Osama bin Laden is dead and that al Qaeda no longer has a presence in Afghanistan or Pakistan. Giraldi accuses U.S. officials of wanting to scare the American public into funding a war on terror to maintain control over the citizenry and to keep high-ranking officials employed. But in reality, concludes

Philip Giraldi, "Looking Beyond Terrorism," CampaignForLiberty.com, October 5, 2009. Copyright © 2009 Campaign For Liberty. Reproduced by permission.

Giraldi, the terrorist threat is more imaginary than real, and thus the war on terror should be ended.

Giraldi is a former CIA counterterrorism specialist and military intelligence officer who served nineteen years overseas in Turkey, Italy, Germany, and Spain.

AS YOU READ, CONSIDER THE FOLLOWING QUESTIONS:
1. Why does the author think Cuba does not belong on the State Department's list of state terrorism sponsors?
2. Why does the author think Syria poses no real threat to the United States?
3. Why does Giraldi think Venezuela should be on the State Department's list? Why is it not?

President Barack Obama has stated that he has a low threshold for "success" in Afghanistan. He wants an Afghanistan that can no longer serve as a base for any terrorist group that would be able to attack the United States. Assuming that the President of the United States is true to his word, he should perhaps consider the possibility that the minimum objective for an American withdrawal from Afghanistan has already been achieved. If that is so, it is time for the United States to end its de facto occupation of the country and leave the Afghan people to settle on a form of government that will satisfy their needs, not those of a segment of the international community led by Washington.

The Threat from Terrorism Is Severely Exaggerated

The fact is that the threat from terrorism has been greatly exaggerated for political reasons to create a sense of fear that has enabled Democrats and Republicans alike to aggrandize power in the federal government. The US State Department issues an annual report that identifies the "state sponsors" of terrorism, those countries that allegedly support and provide a safe haven for terrorist movements. The list has significance because inclusion on it automatically triggers sanctions and other punitive measures, but the report itself and the politics that drive it make its conclusions highly questionable.

A Pumped Up Terrorism List

The current version identifies Cuba, the Sudan, Syria, and Iran as state sponsors but a careful reading of the report itself raises serious questions. The entry on Cuba concedes "Cuba no longer actively supports armed struggle in Latin America and other parts of the world." It justifies Cuba's inclusion on the list by noting that Havana endorses the activities of nominally Marxist Western hemisphere ter-

The Threat from Terrorism Is Very Low

Although dying in a terrorist attack is a scary prospect, statistically Americans are much more likely to die from a plethora of more common dangers, such as driving off the road, being poisoned, and walking down the street. The following chart lists the number of people who died from a variety of ailments and events between 1995 and 2005—terrorism was among the least common causes of death.

SEVERE
Driving off the road: 254,419
Falling: 146,542
Accidental poisoning: 140,327
HIGH
Dying from work: 59,730
Walking down the street: 52,000
Accidentally drowning: 38,302
ELEVATED
Killed by the flu: 19,415
Dying from a hernia: 16,742
GUARDED
Accidental firing of a gun: 8,536
Electrocution: 5,171
LOW
Being shot by law enforcement: 3,949
Terrorism: 3,147
Carbon monoxide in products: 1,554

Taken from: National Highway and Safety Agency, National Vital Statistics Reports, vol. 50, no.15 (09/16/2002), U.S. Consumer Product Safety Commission, the Insurance Information Institute. Compiled in "One Million Ways to Die," *Wired Magazine*, September 11, 2006.

rorist groups like Colombia's FARC [Revolutionary Armed Forces of Colombia]. Does Cuba's encouragement of a terrorist group that it does not actually assist constitute state sponsorship? More important, does Cuba actually threaten the United States through its actions? Or is Cuba on the list because there is a powerful anti-Cuban lobby in Miami? The question answers itself.

Then there is the Sudan, also on the list. The entry on Sudan admits "Sudan remained a cooperative partner in global counterterrorism efforts. During the past year, the Sudanese government continued to pursue terrorist operations directly involving threats to US interests and personnel in Sudan." So why is Sudan listed? Reading the report reveals that Sudan is named because it has not proscribed Hamas [a Palestinian political and paramilitary group], which it considers a legitimate political party in the Palestinian territories and a national liberation movement, a view that is shared by much of the world. Does Sudan threaten the United States or support any group that threatens the United States? No. So one might reasonably question why it is on a terrorism list compiled by the United States Department of State.

> **FAST FACT**
>
> A 2010 CNN poll revealed that 65 percent of Americans are either not too worried or not worried at all that they or a family member will be a victim of a terrorist attack.

No Real Threat to the United States

Syria is also on the State Department list. According to the report, Syria "has not been directly implicated in an act of terrorism since 1986" but the Syrians defend "what they considered to be legitimate armed resistance by Palestinians and Hizballah [an Islamist political and paramilitary group based in Lebanon] against Israeli occupation of Arab territory." As Syria is still technically at war with Israel and Israel occupies Syrian territory this viewpoint should astonish no one. The ongoing hostility means in practice that Syria permits Hamas, Hizballah, and three lesser Palestinian groups to have representational offices in Damascus. Does the existence of the offices of groups that Washington describes at terrorist but which cannot threaten the United States constitute a danger? Of course not. The United States has no legitimate national interest that is in any way threatened by Damascus and the inclusion of Syria on the State Department list is purely political in nature, motivated by disapproval of the regime of President Bashir al-Assad.

And finally there is Iran. Like Syria, Iran undeniably supports Hizballah and Hamas, which it regards as national liberation movements and also as legitimate political parties in Lebanon and in the Palestinian territories. The State Department report also states that Tehran supports both the Afghan Taliban [a Sunni Islamist political group] and Iraqi militants, a contention that is more significant in that it suggests active and ongoing confrontation with US forces in the region. But is the assertion of Iranian involvement true? Many observers believe that Iran's role in Iraq has been greatly exaggerated by the US government, which has needed a scapegoat to explain why the country continues to be experiencing major security problems more than six years after the US invasion. Actual evidence of Iranian involvement is hard to find.

The suggestion that Iran would be aiding the Taliban is even more absurd for sectarian reasons. The Taliban consider Shi'ites [the second largest branch of Islam] like the Iranians to be heretics and has even sanctioned killing them. It has massacred Iranian diplomats in Afghanistan and it would not be an exaggeration to suggest that there is no love lost between the Taliban and Tehran. So again the question must be asked, what is the American horse in this race? As in the case of Syria, does Iran really threaten the United States because it supports two groups that themselves do not endanger the US? There is no American national interest involved and Washington should avoid labeling others as terrorists when it is simultaneously engaged in illegal military action that amounts to state sponsored terrorism in places like Pakistan and Somalia, with whom the US is not at war.

Real Dangers Are Overlooked

One of the real ironies of the State Department's terrorist list is its selectivity. FARC of Colombia is a terrorist group that has actually attacked, killed, and kidnapped Americans. A laptop captured

Some argue that the inclusion of Syria on the U.S. State Department's list of state sponsors of terrorism is motivated more by disapproval of the regime of President Bashir al-Assad (pictured) than by any legitimate threat to the United States.

by Colombian soldiers in March 2008 revealed that the Venezuelan intelligence services were actively negotiating with FARC to provide weapons and other support. Venezuela considers FARC to be a liberation movement, a view not shared by either Washington or Bogota, but perhaps there is another reason why Caracas is not on the state sponsor list. Venezuela provides 11% of the oil consumed in the United States and is the second biggest supplier of crude after only Canada and ahead of Saudi Arabia. If it were to be named a state sponsor of terrorism, buying its oil would become illegal.

An Enemy More Imaginary than Real

And then there are the real terrorists. Al-Qaeda and its truncated leadership is still hiding in a cave in Pakistan with more than 100,000 US and NATO troops camped next door. An increasing number of intelligence analysts and scholars believe that [terrorist] Usama bin Laden is actually dead. General Stanley McChrystal, US Commander in Afghanistan, has admitted that there is no al-Qaeda in Afghanistan. Pakistani sources see little sign of activity directly attributable to al-Qaeda in their own country. They maintain that all of the suicide bombings in Pakistan over the past two years have been carried out by Pakistanis, not by the Arabs or Chechens [a mostly Muslim group that lives in Russia's Caucasus region] normally associated with al-Qaeda. Professor Jean-Pierre Filiu of the highly esteemed French think tank the Paris Institute of Political Studies, sees an al-Qaeda in decline and on the run, reduced to a tiny remnant forced to move frequently and under constant pressure.

Does al-Qaeda threaten the United States? Well, Director of National Intelligence Dennis Blair and Chairman of the Joint Chiefs of Staff Mike Mullen seem to think so, but if they thought otherwise they would be out of a job. Perhaps the American public should begin to ask why hundreds of billions of dollars are being spent yearly to fight an enemy that might well be more imaginary that real. It is not unreasonable to suggest that it is time to put the genie back into the bottle and end the global war on terror once and for all. If President Obama really believes what he says, it is past time for him to accept that Afghanistan is a mess but unlikely to become a terrorist haven. Which means "mission accomplished" and it's time to leave.

EVALUATING THE AUTHOR'S ARGUMENTS:

Giraldi is a former counterterrorism specialist who worked for the Central Intelligence Agency (CIA). Does knowing his background influence your opinion of his argument? Are you more likely to agree with his assessment of the threat posed by terrorism because of his professional experience? Why or why not?

Terrorists Are Likely to Acquire Nuclear Weapons

Graham Allison

"The chances of a nuclear terrorist attack in the next decade are greater than 50 percent."

In the following viewpoint Graham Allison argues that terrorists are likely to acquire nuclear weapons. He explains that some of the country's foremost thinkers believe such an event is inevitable and warn the risk grows greater with every passing year. Allison claims terrorists are determined to attack the United States with a nuclear weapon. He suggests they might either steal the materials needed to build a weapon or buy them from a rogue nation such as North Korea or Pakistan. Allison argues the chance of terrorists getting their hands on a nuclear weapon in the next decade is at least 50 percent; but even if it was only 1 percent, the consequences of such an attack would be unimaginably horrific. For this reason, he urges authorities to do everything possible to prevent the scenario from becoming reality.

Allison is the director of the Belfer Center for Science and International Affairs and a professor at Harvard University's John F. Kennedy School of Government.

AS YOU READ, CONSIDER THE FOLLOWING QUESTIONS:

1. What did Richard Garwin tell Congress in March 2007, according to Allison?
2. What does Allison say al-Qaeda's leadership is "singularly focused" on?
3. What is the Nuclear Non-Proliferation Treaty and what benefits does Allison say it has had?

"Radioactive hype" [an article] by John Mueller sharpens the barbs from his recent book, *Overblown*, in ways that demonstrate that he is, above all, a committed contrarian. One can agree with many points in his article and book. But his central propositions about the danger and appropriate responses to terrorism, nuclear terrorism and the proliferation of nuclear weapons are profoundly mistaken. . . .

The Nuclear Threat Is Real and Dangerous

Mueller is entitled to his opinion that the threat of nuclear proliferation and nuclear terrorism is "exaggerated" and "overwrought." But analysts of various political persuasions, in and out of government, are virtually unanimous in their judgment to the contrary. As the national-security community learned during the Cold War, risk = likelihood x consequences. Thus, even when the likelihood of nuclear Armageddon was small, the consequences were so catastrophic that prudent policymakers felt a categorical imperative to do everything that feasibly could be done to prevent that war. Today, a single nuclear bomb exploding in just one city would change our world. Given such consequences, differences between a 1 percent and a 20 percent likelihood of such an attack are relatively insignificant when considering how we should respond to the threat.

Richard Garwin, a designer of the hydrogen bomb who [Italian physicist] Enrico Fermi once called "the only true genius I had ever met," told Congress in March [2007] that he estimated a "20 percent per year probability [of a nuclear explosion—not just a contaminated, dirty bomb—a nuclear explosion] with American cities and European cities included." My Harvard colleague Matthew Bunn has created a model in the *Annals of the American Academy of Political and Social Science* that estimates the probability of a nuclear terrorist attack over a ten-year period to be 29 percent—identical to the average estimate from a poll of security experts commissioned by Senator Richard Lugar in 2005. My book, *Nuclear Terrorism*, states my own best judgment that, on the current trend line, the chances of a nuclear terrorist attack in the next decade are greater than 50 percent. Former Secretary of Defense William Perry has expressed his own view that my work may even underestimate the risk. Warren Buffet, the world's most successful investor and legendary odds-maker in pricing insurance policies for unlikely but catastrophic events, concluded that nuclear terrorism is "inevitable." He stated, "I don't see any way that it won't happen."

> ## FAST FACT
>
> On October 9, 2006, North Korea—a former signatory to the Nuclear Non-Proliferation Treaty—tested its first nuclear bomb. North Korea is believed to possess enough highly enriched uranium to make between six and ten small nuclear weapons and has threatened on numerous occasions to sell such technology to terrorists.

Al-Qaeda Seeks Nuclear Weapons

To assess the threat one must answer five core questions: who, what, where, when and how?

Who could be planning a nuclear terrorist attack? [The Islamist terrorist group] Al-Qaeda remains the leading candidate. According to the most recent National Intelligence Estimate (NIE), Al-Qaeda has been substantially reconstituted—but with its leadership having moved from a medieval Afghanistan to Pakistan—a nation that actually has nuclear weapons. As former CIA Director George J. Tenet's memoir reports, Al-Qaeda's leadership has remained "singularly focused on acquiring WMDs [weapons of mass destruction]" and that the main

How Terrorists Might Acquire Nuclear Weapons

Nuclear weapons are difficult to come by, but experts worry that terrorists might buy, steal, or build their own. The following diagram explores one path for such an event.

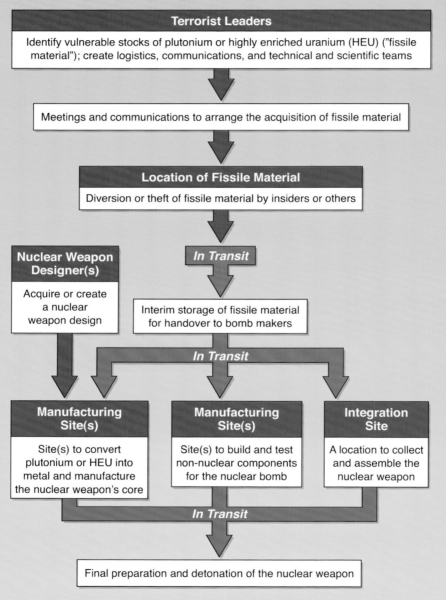

Terrorist Leaders

Identify vulnerable stocks of plutonium or highly enriched uranium (HEU) ("fissile material"); create logistics, communications, and technical and scientific teams

Meetings and communications to arrange the acquisition of fissile material

Location of Fissile Material

Diversion or theft of fissile material by insiders or others

In Transit

Nuclear Weapon Designer(s)

Acquire or create a nuclear weapon design

Interim storage of fissile material for handover to bomb makers

In Transit

Manufacturing Site(s)

Site(s) to convert plutonium or HEU into metal and manufacture the nuclear weapon's core

Manufacturing Site(s)

Site(s) to build and test non-nuclear components for the nuclear bomb

Integration Site

A location to collect and assemble the nuclear weapon

In Transit

Final preparation and detonation of the nuclear weapon

Taken from: David Albright, "Terrorists' Acquisition of Nuclear Weapons: The Dangerous Synergy Between Weak States and Illicit Nuclear Procurement," Institute for Science and International Security, 2006, p.12.

threat is the nuclear one." Tenet concluded, "I am convinced that this is where [Osama bin Laden] and his operatives want to go."

What nuclear weapons could terrorists use? A ready-made weapon from the arsenal of one of the nuclear-weapons states or an elementary nuclear bomb constructed from highly enriched uranium made by a state remain most likely. As John Foster, a leading U.S. bomb-maker and former director of the Lawrence Livermore National Laboratory, wrote a quarter of a century ago, "If the essential nuclear materials are at hand, it is possible to make an atomic bomb using information that is available in the open literature."

No Doubt About Terrorists' Abilities

Where could terrorists acquire a nuclear bomb? If a nuclear attack occurs, Russia will be the most likely source of the weapon or material. A close second, however, is North Korea, which now has ten bombs worth of plutonium, or Pakistan with sixty nuclear bombs. Finally, research reactors in forty developing and transitional countries still hold the essential ingredient for nuclear weapons.

When could terrorists launch the first nuclear attack? If terrorists bought or stole a nuclear weapon in good working condition, they could explode it today. If terrorists acquired one hundred pounds of highly enriched uranium, they could make a working elementary nuclear bomb in less than a year.

How could terrorists deliver a nuclear weapon to its target? In the same way that illegal items come to our cities every day. As one of my former colleagues has quipped, if you have any doubt about the ability of terrorists to deliver a weapon to an American target, remember: They could hide it in a bale of marijuana.

No Exaggeration or Overreaction

Readers of Mueller's judgment that policies aimed at preventing proliferation have been "obsessive" and "counterproductive" should be aware of his criteria for what constitutes an "overreaction." In *Overblown*, he argues that America's reaction to [the December 7, 1941, Japanese attack on] Pearl Harbor was exaggerated. America's overreaction led it to declare war on Japan, when a policy of "military containment and harassment" would have been sufficient to pressure Japan to withdraw from its empire.

Mueller's claim that the quest to control proliferation has been "substantively counterproductive" misunderstands the impact successful policy has had in preventing what would have been catastrophic outcomes. Mueller takes to task President John Kennedy's 1962 prediction that if states acquired nuclear weapons at the rate they achieved the technical ability to build bombs, there could be twenty nuclear powers by 1975. He argues the claim was exaggerated simply because it did not happen. But the purpose of Kennedy's warning was to awaken the world to the unacceptable dangers of unconstrained nuclear proliferation. The United States' and other nations' refusal to accept those consequences motivated an international initiative to create the non-proliferation regime, the centerpiece of which is the Nuclear Non-Proliferation Treaty (NPT). Thanks to this regime, 183 nations, including scores that have the technical capability to build nuclear arsenals, have renounced nuclear weapons. Four decades later, there are only eight and a half nuclear-weapons states, not twenty or forty. (North Korea is the only self-declared but unrecognized nuclear state.)

The gravest challenges to the non-proliferation regime today are North Korea and Iran. If each succeeds in becoming a nuclear-weapons state, we are likely to witness the unraveling of the non-proliferation regime and a cascade of proliferation. As [former secretary of state] Henry Kissinger recently said, "there is no greater challenge to the global nuclear order today than the impending proliferation of nuclear weapons and the increasing likelihood that terrorists may conduct a nuclear 9/11."

EVALUATING THE AUTHOR'S ARGUMENTS:

Graham Allison quotes from several sources to support the points he makes in his essay. Make a list of all the sources he quotes, including their credentials and the nature of their comments. Then, analyze his sources—are they credible? Are they well qualified to speak on this subject? To which of Allison's arguments and ideas do the quotes lend support?

Terrorists Are Not Likely to Acquire Nuclear Weapons

John Mueller

"Any notion that al-Qaeda is likely to come up with nuclear weapons looks far fetched in the extreme."

In the following viewpoint John Mueller argues that the chances of terrorists acquiring and using nuclear weapons is slim to none. He claims most of the reports that feature terrorists buying or seeking nuclear weapons materials have turned out to be entirely false, based on rumor, or from sources that are not credible. He says there is very little hard, credible evidence that terrorists have obtained nuclear weapons or that they even have interest in doing so. Mueller says if terrorists could get such weapons they would have used them in an attack by now. The fact that they have not is proof for Mueller that it is probably very difficult for terrorists to acquire nuclear weapons, and he therefore urges Americans to be cautious but not hysterical about this issue.

Mueller is a professor of political science at Ohio State University and the author of *Atomic Obsession: Nuclear Alarmism from Hiroshima to Al Qaeda.*

According to Defense Secretary Robert Gates, every senior government leader is kept awake at night by "the thought of a terrorist ending up with a weapon of mass destruction, especially nuclear."

This is, I suppose, understandable. It was in 1995 that the thoughtful analyst Graham Allison declared that "in the absence of a determined program of action, we have every reason to anticipate acts of nuclear terrorism against American targets before this decade is out." Unabashed, he maintained in an influential 2004 book [*Nuclear Terrorism*] that "on the current path, a nuclear terrorist attack on America in the decade ahead is more likely than not." And it was on *60 Minutes*, on Nov. 14, 2004, that former CIA analyst Michael Scheuer assured his rapt interviewer that the explosion of a nuclear or dirty bomb in the United States was "probably a near thing."

In contrast to such bold proclamations, the evidence about the degree to which al-Qaeda—the only Islamic terrorist organization that targets the U.S. homeland—has pursued, or even had much interest in, a nuclear-weapons program is limited and often ambiguous. Still, the shards that exist have been routinely parlayed and exaggerated by a parade of official and unofficial alarmists.

Scant Evidence That Terrorists Even Want Nuclear Weapons

For example, in 2004, the 9/11 Commission [an independent bipartisan commission that prepared a complete report of the circumstances surrounding the September 11, 2001, terrorist attacks] insisted that "al-Qaeda has tried to acquire or make nuclear weapons for at least ten years." The only substantial evidence it provided for this assertion comes from an episode that supposedly took place around 1993 in Sudan, when [al-Qaeda leader] Osama bin Laden's aides were scammed as they tried to buy some uranium. Information about this caper apparently came entirely from Jamal al-Fadl, who defected from al-Qaeda in 1996 after he had been caught stealing $110,000 from the organization. He tried selling his story around the Middle East, but only the Americans were buying. In his prize-winning *The Looming Tower*, Lawrence Wright relays the testimony of the man who allegedly purchased the substance for bin Laden, as well as that of a Sudanese intelligence agent. Both assert that, although there were various other scams going around at the time that may have served as grist for Fadl, the uranium episode never happened. It's possible, of course, that Fadl—a "lovable rogue" who is "fixated on money" and "likes to please," according to an FBI debriefer—is telling the truth, or at least what he thinks is the truth. But his allegations, now endlessly repeated, have gone from a color-ful story relayed by an admitted embezzler on the lam to unques-

> ## FAST FACT
>
> World stockpiles of nuclear weapons have declined by more than two-thirds since the 1960s. About twenty-seven thousand active nuclear weapons remain worldwide; 95 percent of these belong to the United States and Russia.

tioned fact. We know, it is repeatedly declared, that bin Laden tried to purchase weapons-grade uranium in Sudan. Qualifications, even modest ones, concerning the veracity of the evidence behind that declaration have vanished in the retelling.

Al-Qaeda Has Not Invested in WMDs

Various sources suggest that there were radical elements in bin Laden's entourage interested in pursuing atomic weapons or other weapons of mass destruction when the group was in Afghanistan in the 1990s. Yet the same sources indicate that bin Laden essentially sabotaged the idea by refusing to fund a WMD [weapons of mass destruction] project or even initiate planning for one. Analyst Anne Stenersen notes that evidence from a recovered al-Qaeda computer shows that only some $2,000 to $4,000 was earmarked for WMD research, apparently for very crude chemical work to make biological weapons. For comparison, she points out that the millennial [Japanese] terrorist group Aum Shinrikyo appears to have invested $30 million into manufacturing sarin gas [a human-made chemical warfare agent].

To show al-Qaeda's desire to obtain atomic weapons, many have focused on a set of conversations that took place in Afghanistan in August 2001 between two Pakistani nuclear scientists, bin Laden, and three other al-Qaeda officials. Pakistani intelligence officers characterize the discussions as "academic." Reports suggest that bin Laden may have had access to some radiological material—acquired for him by radical Islamists in Uzbekistan—but the scientists told him that he could not manufacture a weapon with it. Bin Laden's questions do not seem to have been very sophisticated. The scientists were incapable of providing truly helpful information because their expertise was not in bomb design but in processing fissile material, which is almost certainly beyond the capacities of a non-state group. Nonetheless, some U.S. intelligence agencies convinced themselves that the scientist provided al-Qaeda with a "blueprint" for constructing nuclear weapons.

Rumors and Reports but No Credible Proof

Khalid Sheikh Mohammed, the apparent mastermind behind the 9/11 attacks, reportedly said that al-Qaeda's atom-bomb efforts never went beyond searching the Internet. After the fall of the Taliban [a Sunni Islamist political movement] in 2001, technical experts from the CIA and the Department of Energy examined information uncovered in Afghanistan and came to similar conclusions. They found no credible proof that al-Qaeda had obtained fissile material or a nuclear weapon and no evidence of "any radioactive material suitable for weapons." They did uncover, however, a "nuclear related" document discussing "openly available concepts about the nuclear fuel cycle and some weapons related issues." Physicist and weapons expert David Albright concludes that any al-Qaeda atomic efforts were "seriously disrupted"—indeed, "nipped in the bud"—by the invasion of

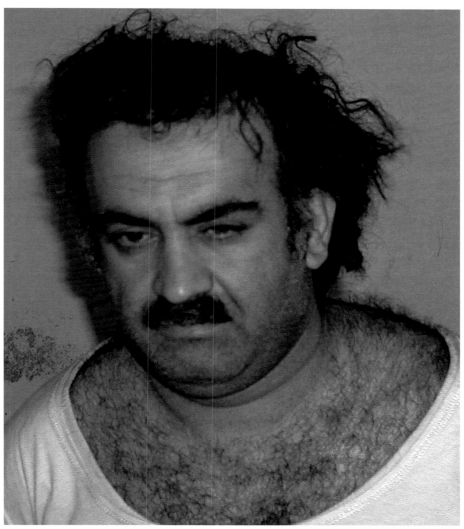

Khalid Sheikh Mohammed, mastermind of the 9/11 attack on the United States, revealed under interrogation that al-Qaeda's efforts to obtain a nuclear device never went beyond searching the Internet.

Afghanistan in 2001. After that, the "chance of al-Qaeda detonating a nuclear explosive appears on reflection to be low."

Rumors and reports that al-Qaeda has managed to purchase an atomic bomb, or several, have been around now for over a decade. One story alleges that bin Laden gave a group of Chechens $30 million in cash and two tons of opium in exchange for 20 nuclear warheads. If any of these reports were true, one might think the terrorist group (or its supposed Chechen suppliers) would have tried to set off one of those things by now or that al-Qaeda would have left some trace of the weapons behind in Afghanistan after its hasty exit in 2001. . . .

Experts Have Exaggerated the Threat

When examined, the signs of al-Qaeda's desire to go atomic and its progress in accomplishing that exceedingly difficult task are remarkably vague, if not negligible. After an exhaustive study of available materials, Stenersen finds that, although al-Qaeda central may have considered nuclear and other non-conventional weapons, there "is little evidence that such ideas ever developed into actual plans, or that they were given any kind of priority at the expense of more traditional types of terrorist attacks." There is no reason to believe, moreover, that the group's chances improved after they were forcefully expelled from their comparatively unembattled base in Afghanistan.

Glenn Carle, a 23-year veteran of the Central Intelligence Agency, where he was deputy national intelligence officer for transnational threats, warns about taking "fright at the specter our leaders have exaggerated" and argues that we should "see jihadists for the small, lethal, disjointed and miserable opponents that they are." Terrorism specialist Bruce Hoffman remains quite worried about loose terrorist networks, but he also points out that they are likely to be "less sophisticated" and "less technically competent" than earlier terrorists.

Nuclear Weapons Hysteria

In 1996, one of terrorism studies' top gurus, Walter Laqueur, insisted that some terrorist groups "almost certainly" will use weapons of mass destruction "in the foreseeable future." What was then the foreseeable future is presumably now history. In today's reality, terrorists seem to be heeding the advice found in a memo on an al-Qaeda laptop seized in Pakistan in 2004: "Make use of that which is available . . . rather than waste valuable time becoming despondent over that which is not within our reach." That is: keep it simple, stupid. Although there have been plenty of terrorist attacks in the world since 2001, all—thus far, at least—have relied on conventional destructive methods.

There hasn't even been much in the way of gas bombings, even in Iraq where the technology is hardly a secret.

In sum, any notion that al-Qaeda is likely to come up with nuclear weapons looks far fetched in the extreme. We still have reason for concern or at least for watchfulness. But hysteria—not to mention sleeplessness—is hardly called for.

EVALUATING THE AUTHORS' ARGUMENTS:

Graham Allison and John Mueller disagree with each other over whether terrorists are likely to acquire nuclear weapons. In your opinion, which author made the better argument? Why? List at least four pieces of evidence (quotes, statistics, facts, or statements of reasoning) that caused you to side with one author over the other.

Terrorists Are Likely to Acquire Biological Weapons

Bob Graham

"There is little reason to believe that the lethal pathogens of Pokrov [research center] are secure from falling into terrorist hands."

It would be easy for terrorists to steal and deploy biological weapons argues Bob Graham in the following viewpoint. He describes his experience at a Russian research facility where he saw deadly biological materials stored poorly and unsafely. Graham says it would be easy to steal these pathogens from the facility, which had open doors, a shoddy security system, and important classified information lying about. Graham says these and other insecure facilities make it possible—and probable—for terrorists to steal biological weapons material and launch a deadly attack on the United States. In fact, Graham says a biological weapons attack is more likely than a nuclear one. The United States has poured billions of dollars into securing nuclear stockpiles but has not put the same effort into securing biological materials, which Graham says could be just as deadly if used in an attack. For all of these reasons he urges American officials to do everything possible to reduce the risk that lethal bacteria, viruses, and other pathogens will fall into the hands of terrorists.

Graham was the governor of Florida from 1979 to 1987 and a U.S. senator from 1987 to 2005. He currently also serves as chairman of the Commission on Weapons of Mass Destruction Proliferation and Terrorism.

AS YOU READ, CONSIDER THE FOLLOWING QUESTIONS:
1. What does Graham say note cards and strings were used for at the Pokrov research center?
2. What was the conclusion of the World at Risk report, according to Graham?
3. How many U.S. scientists does Graham say are authorized to work with bioterrorism materials? What makes him nervous about this?

I n May 2002, I visited Pokrov, a largely abandoned Soviet-era agricultural research center east of Moscow. Originally established to produce vaccines for animals, Pokrov became a laboratory for biological weapons, especially anthrax [an acute infectious disease caused by spore-forming bacteria], in the final years of the Cold War.

We entered the building, which stored samples of all the materials produced at Pokrov. The woven wire and electrified fence that at one time had secured the building was a fallen, rusting heap. The security alarm to the main entrance had been turned off and the door was ajar.

Biological Materials Are Not Secured

Up two flights of steel-grate stairs were the storage rooms, two tennis court–sized rooms filled with commercial refrigerators. Several refrigerators had two common features: note cards listing the materials inside and flimsy strings encircling them. Our hosts explained that a broken string would indicate that someone had possibly opened the refrigerator and stolen the materials inside.

I left Pokrov without much confidence in the security afforded the most lethal biological materials in the world.

The Risk from a Biological Weapons Attack Is Grave

Earlier this month [December 2008], the Commission on Weapons of Mass Destruction Proliferation and Terrorism, which I chaired, presented its final report, *World at Risk*, to President [George W.] Bush, Vice President–elect Joe Biden and congressional leaders.

The report concluded that "unless the world community acts decisively and with great urgency, it is more likely than not that a weapon of mass destruction will be used in a terrorist attack somewhere in the world by the end of 2013."

But the type of catastrophe may be a surprise to some. In fact: "Terrorists are more likely to be able to obtain and use a biological weapon than a nuclear weapon."

> **FAST FACT**
>
> In 2010 Jeffrey Lockwood, professor of entomology at the University of Wyoming and author of *Six-Legged Soldiers: Using Insects as Weapons of War*, warned it would be relatively easy for terrorists to launch a biological terrorist attack using swarms of insects to spread a disease such as Rift Valley Fever, which can cause sickness and death.

Imagining the Consequences

The closest the United States has come to a bioterrorist attack was in October 2001, when letters contaminated with anthrax bacterial spores were mailed to two senators, a television anchorman and an employee of the *National Enquirer*.

Seven letters were mailed, containing less than 15 teaspoons of anthrax. This miniscule quantity resulted in five deaths, placed 30,000 people at risk, closed government buildings for months and produced economic damage estimated at $6 billion.

It isn't hard to imagine the consequences in death, destruction, panic, and dollars of a large-scale biological attack using anthrax spores manufactured from a vial like those in the refrigerators at Pokrov.

An Explosion in Biological Dangers

Biological materials are more ubiquitous and less secure than nuclear.

Since the fall of the Soviet Union, the United States and its allies have wisely expended tens of billions of dollars to identify, capture, and secure nuclear materials.

The same cannot be said for lethal pathogens. The United States has cut back its biological threat reduction programs in Russia, and the Russians have refused greater transparency at their Ministry of Defense controlled biological weapons facilities. There is little reason to believe that the lethal pathogens of Pokrov are secure from falling into terrorist hands.

While the rugged and persistent anthrax spores remain the pathogen of first resort, the last two decades have seen an explosion of biological dangers.

No Comprehensive Regulation

Since 9/11, the federal government has poured billions into defensive research on pathogens that might be used for bioterrorism.

There are now 14,000 U.S. scientists authorized to work on these materials, increasing the risk of a few bad apples with access. Shockingly, there continues to be no comprehensive regulation within

Bob Graham and other members of the Weapons of Mass Destruction Proliferation and Terrorism Commission report their findings to Congress on the terrorist threat to the United States.

HON. BOB GRAHAM   HON. JIM TALENT   HON. TIM ROEMER   ROBIN CLEVELAND

the United States or internationally of the sites where lethal pathogens are produced or of the scientists capable of their production.

Al Qaeda Wants to Attack

[The Islamist terrorist group] Al Qaeda remains intent on securing lethal pathogens for use against the United States. Agents of [terrorist] Osama bin Laden have been intercepted attempting to procure biological capabilities and materials in Europe and Asia.

The laboratories we discovered in Kandahar after the October 2001 invasion of Afghanistan have been relocated to the tribal areas of Pakistan. As Richard Danzig, former secretary of the navy, has observed, "Only a thin wall of terrorists' ignorance and inexperience now protects us."

Nuclear terrorism has been described as the ultimate preventable catastrophe. We hope so, and we also hope and believe our commission report has created a roadmap for significantly reducing the risk that the worst bacteria and viruses will fall into the hands of the worst terrorists and nations.

EVALUATING THE AUTHOR'S ARGUMENTS:

Graham is a former governor and senator. His current job is to head a commission that is responsible for reporting to the president on the risks of weapons of mass destruction and terrorism. Does knowing Graham's professional background influence your opinion of his argument? Does it make you more likely to believe him about the threat from biological weapons? Why or why not?

Terrorists Are Not Likely to Acquire Biological Weapons

William R. Clark

"'It is almost inconceivable that any terrorist organization . . . could on their own develop, from scratch, a bioweapon capable of causing mass casualties on American soil.'"

In the following viewpoint William R. Clark argues that terrorists are not likely to attack the United States with biological weapons. Clark says attacks using biological weapons are notoriously unsuccessful—although some viruses and bacteria are very dangerous, they would likely be weakened or destroyed in the attack itself. Clark thinks terrorists are incapable of making bioweapons themselves; developing weapons-grade biological pathogens requires years of training and a level of skill Clark says terrorists just do not have. Furthermore, Clark does not see why terrorists would invest the time and research into making a bioweapon when they could simply carry out a 9/11-style attack with much less time, research, skill, and planning. Clark concludes that fighting bioterrorism is a waste of time and money, both of which he says

Matt Palmquist, "Bioterror in Context: How and Why the Threat of Bioterrorism Has Been So Greatly Exaggerated: An Interview of UCLA's William R. Clark," Miller-McCune.com, May 19, 2008. Copyright © 2008 Miller-McCune Inc. Reproduced by permission.

would be better spent on fighting global warming or a natural disease outbreak.

Clark, a research scientist with over thirty years experience, is professor of immunology at the University of California at Los Angeles. He is also the author of the book *Bracing for Armageddon?*

AS YOU READ, CONSIDER THE FOLLOWING QUESTIONS:
1. What does Clark say was the result of the 1984 bioattack by the Rajneesh cult in Oregon?
2. What is the difference, according to Clark, between a bioterrorism attack and a natural pandemic? Why does he think a pandemic is more dangerous?
3. What is a "push package," and why does Clark think it would not work in the event of a successful bioterror attack?

Although the United States will have spent $50 billion on defense against a bioterrorism attack by the end of 2008, [Professor William R.] Clark argues that we have much more to fear from natural pandemic outbreaks, such as the viruses causing SARS and H5N1 avian flu. He reviews all the worst-case bioterror scenarios—from agricultural terrorism to poisoning the water supply; from genetically engineered pathogens to the Centers for Disease Control and Prevention's official list of bioterrorist weapons—and writes: "It is almost inconceivable that any terrorist organization we know of in the world today, foreign or domestic, could on their own develop, from scratch, a bioweapon capable of causing mass casualties on American soil."

A History of Failed Bioterror Attacks

Clark chronicles the few (failed) attempts at launching large-scale bioterror attacks, beginning with the Rajneesh cult in Oregon, which slipped salmonella into salad bars in an attempt to influence a local election in 1984; the cult's efforts sickened more than 700 people but killed none. The Aum Shinrikyo cult in Japan earned worldwide headlines in 1995 for releasing sarin nerve gas into the Tokyo subway system, killing 12 people. But this was a chemical attack, and despite millions of dollars in funding and a staff of scientists, Aum Shinrikyo's several attempts at producing biological weapons, including the development of a relatively harmless anthrax strain normally used for animal vaccinations, produced no significant casualties. In the early 1990s, a militia group called the Minnesota Patriots Council made some ricin—a potent poison derived from castor beans—and stored it in a jar but never figured out how to use it. And the 2001 postal anthrax attacks spurred the government to develop a host of expensive countermeasures that are, Clark writes, largely unnecessary. These include the creation of a Strategic National Stockpile of vaccines and antidotes; the CDC's "push packages," cargo containers weighing a total of 94 tons whose medicine contents are constantly replenished and ready to be shipped to an emergency site. . . .

Miller-McCune talked to Clark about his book and his rather reassuring overview of the bioterror threat.

Bioterrorism Is Not Practical

Miller-McCune: When did you begin suspecting that our bioterrorism fears might be a tad exaggerated?

William Clark: The more I looked into it, I thought, Jeez, what are these guys talking about? What are the odds that a terrorist group, no matter how well financed, would be able to create a bioterror weapon? I began looking into what it takes to really make a successful bioterrorism agent, and I just became very skeptical of this whole thing. The (United States) military gave up bioweapons 30 years ago. They're too undependable; they're too hard to use; they're too hard to make. Then I started checking around, and I found there's a whole literature out there of people who've been screaming for years that this whole bioterrorism thing is really overblown; it's not practical; it's never going to work. Aum Shinrikyo couldn't get it to work; those guys put millions and millions of dollars into it. So you think of a bunch of guys sitting in a cave in Afghanistan—they're sure as hell not going to do it. Is any government going to do it? No. So that made me very skeptical, and I went back to Oxford and said, "This whole thing's a crock." . . .

The kind of an organization you'd have to put together, with the varying expertise that is required to make one of these things and

Hazardous materials workers prepare to enter a postal facility in response to anthrax contamination. Such response plans are expensive and elaborate, and some argue they are unnecessary.

deploy it, takes a whole group of people with all kinds of different skills, from engineers to meteorologists. That's just not going to happen. You can run an airplane into an office tower, and you get instant everything you could ever possibly hope for. So why would anybody sit around for years and years? The Aum Shinrikyo guys tried for six, seven years and couldn't get it to work. And a lot of them had Ph.D.s.

Doomsday Scenarios Have Been Exaggerated

But you start the book with the Dark Winter scenario, a simulated smallpox outbreak that was performed in June 2001 for 50 government officials at Andrews Air Force Base. This was an exercise staged by several prestigious institutes and government agencies, and it paints an awfully grim portrait of our ability to counter the outbreak, with 100,000 deaths forecast and 1.6 million people coming in contact with smallpox. Was that the scariest thing you stumbled across?

Absolutely. As soon as I read that, I said, "Sign me up, I'm going to join the Army." But then, following through on it, I saw the number of people out there who had been basically debunking it—at higher government levels, in scientific journals, think tanks, white papers—and the government just blew them off. I spent a whole year and a half backtracking on Dark Winter, and I realized this is an industry. There are about a dozen of these exercises or workshops, and they scare the crap out of politicians, who go to these things and realize how little they know. I mean, look, some good stuff has come out of it; there's no doubt about that. Public health has been upgraded; communications among people who would be managing an attack like that have been improved. But I think there's a hell of a lot more to worry about from an avian influenza pandemic, by a factor of 100 or so. They're very different situations. A bioterrorism attack is something that happens in a specific locality and requires a certain response, whereas pandemics just spread all over the whole freakin' country. . . .

These (terrorists) want immediate impact on television. The Dark Winter scenario is pretty graphic television, but the smallpox vaccines that are on hand now make it unlikely. That Dark Winter scenario really stretched things, cherry-picking some of the worst-case scenarios. So many experts have torn that thing apart. The idea that each person infected would infect 20 to 30 other people—that's just not realistic. They'd be quarantined immediately. . . .

> **FAST FACT**
>
> The Center for International and Strategic Studies reports that Iran has had biological weapons since 1990 or earlier. Yet it has never shared or sold the technology to any terrorist group, even the ones to which it has provided funding and other weaponry.

Bioterror Countermeasures Are Ineffective

I did want to ask about some of the countermeasures the United States has developed. For instance, these 12 push packages, which are stashed in secret, climate-controlled locations. All states have to have a dedicated, 12,000-square-foot facility to be ready for one of these push packages . . .

I talked to people here in Los Angeles County who are involved in managing the county's response to a bioterrorism attack. They're not too impressed by push packages.

Oh, really. Why not?

The problem is they re not just for bioterror; they're loaded with antidotes for nuclear, chemical, all kinds of events. These are enormously complex packages. By the time you sorted through that damn thing and figured out where the stuff was, there's no time. I mean, these people have to organize cops and firefighters and paramedics and doctors and nurses—boom, boom, boom. We don't have time to be dealing with a 94-ton push package. I think the government is starting to worry a little about the cost of maintaining these things because there are so many medicines and drugs in there that have different shelf lives. They have to be replaced periodically, and that's expensive. . . .

Terrorists Do Not Have the Skills

So you mention that this book became political as you explored the subject. Did you go into the project having a particular political slant?

Only that as a scientist, I thought, "You've gotta be kidding me" [that terrorists could develop their own bioweapon]. Who's gonna have the combined expertise from so many areas—microbiology, bioengineering—so many things? I've spent all my life in a lab as a scientist. Things are just not that easy to do. They're bloody hard. If you're at a place like UCLA, you've got 500 other people around you, so you can usually solve a problem. But for a person working on their own, not in a university environment, I just don't see how they can do that.

There Are Much Greater Threats Than Bioterrorism

But we've spent $50 billion against bioterrorism.

Yeah, $50 billion. And there has been some spillover. We're better prepared for a pandemic because what they're doing for bioterror would also prepare us somewhat for a pandemic attack. It's the tail wagging the dog. Before, bioterrorism was the dog and pandemics were the tail; now it's the other way around. Pandemics are now the dog, and you get a little bit of spillover to help in a bioterror attack.

So the mindset is changing?

I think so. Some of the more sober, sophisticated, knowledgeable scientists have been looking into this a bit more deeply, realizing that while they may not be entirely convinced that bioterrorism is not a threat, they're starting to get the notion that avian influenza—or some other natural outbreak—is almost a slam-dunk. We get two or three of those a century, historically, as far back as we have records. There are these outbreaks of natural human pathogens that wreak utter havoc. . . . So those numbers start to sink in, and we've spent $50 billion on something that's killed five people. Influenza could kill tens of thousands at the very least.

And I hope . . . to keep the pressure going on the government to pay more attention to things that present a much more serious threat to us, like infectious diseases or global warming.

EVALUATING THE AUTHORS' ARGUMENTS:

In the previous viewpoint Bob Graham warned that if terrorists attacked with biological weapons they could cause wide-scale death, destruction, panic, and do millions of dollars in damage. List at least three specific reasons why William R. Clark would say he thinks such a scenario is not likely to occur. Write one paragraph for each reason. Then, state with which author you ultimately agree on whether a biological terrorist attack is likely.

Chapter 2

What Should the United States Do to Prevent Terrorism?

Afghans and U.S. Marines discuss compensation for damage inflicted on a house in Dahaneh, Afghanistan. There is debate over whether the U.S. mission in Afghanistan is a cause of terrorism or its cure.

Fighting the War in Afghanistan Can Prevent Terrorism

"Our security is at stake in Afghanistan. . . . This is the epicenter of violent extremism practiced by al Qaeda."

Barack Obama

Barack Obama is the forty-fourth president of the United States. In the following speech he outlines why he believes fighting the war in Afghanistan can prevent terrorism. He explains that America's war on terror started in Afghanistan—it was in this country where the September 11 hijackers trained and where al Qaeda leader Osama bin Laden was given shelter by the Taliban government. After September 11 the United States successfully ousted the Taliban from power and captured or killed many terrorists. But since then, Obama says, the United States has neglected Afghanistan, and terrorists have once again started to take root there. Obama warns that Afghanistan could easily become another safe haven for terrorists, a place from which they could plot more attacks. For these reasons, Obama concludes the war in Afghanistan is central

Barack Obama, "Remarks by the President in Address to the Nation on the Way Forward in Afghanistan and Pakistan," WhiteHouse.gov, December 1, 2009. Reproduced by permission.

to America's national security, and this is why he committed additional troops to the war there.

AS YOU READ, CONSIDER THE FOLLOWING QUESTIONS:
1. What does Obama say the United States achieved within a matter of months of going to war in Afghanistan?
2. In what ways does Obama say Afghanistan has moved backward? List at least two ways.
3. How many additional troops does Obama say were committed to Afghanistan as a result of the deteriorating security situation there?

I t's important to recall why America and our allies were compelled to fight a war in Afghanistan in the first place. We did not ask for this fight.

The War on Terror Began in Afghanistan

On September 11, 2001, 19 men hijacked four airplanes and used them to murder nearly 3,000 people. They struck at our military and economic nerve centers. They took the lives of innocent men, women, and children without regard to their faith or race or station. Were it not for the heroic actions of passengers onboard one of those flights, they could have also struck at one of the great symbols of our democracy in Washington, and killed many more.

As we know, these men belonged to al Qaeda—a group of extremists who have distorted and defiled Islam, one of the world's great religions, to justify the slaughter of innocents. Al Qaeda's base of operations was in Afghanistan, where they were harbored by the Taliban—a ruthless, repressive and radical movement that seized control of that country after it was ravaged by years of Soviet occupation and civil war, and after the attention of America and our friends had turned elsewhere.

A Promising Start

Just days after 9/11, Congress authorized the use of force against al Qaeda and those who harbored them—an authorization that continues to this day. The vote in the Senate was 98 to nothing. The vote in the House was 420 to 1. For the first time in its history, the North Atlantic Treaty Organization invoked Article 5—the commitment that says an attack on one member nation is an attack on all. And the United Nations Security Council endorsed the use of all necessary steps to respond to the 9/11 attacks. America, our allies and the world were acting as one to destroy al Qaeda's terrorist network and to protect our common security.

President Barack Obama speaks to West Point cadets about his way forward in the war in Afghanistan.

Under the banner of this domestic unity and international legitimacy—and only after the Taliban refused to turn over [terrorist] Osama bin Laden—we sent our troops into Afghanistan. Within a matter of months, al Qaeda was scattered and many of its operatives were killed. The Taliban was driven from power and pushed back on its heels. A place that had known decades of fear now had reason to hope. At a conference convened by the U.N., a provisional government was established under President Hamid Karzai. And an International Security Assistance Force was established to help bring a lasting peace to a war-torn country.

Then, in early 2003, the decision was made to wage a second war, in Iraq. The wrenching debate over the Iraq war is well-known

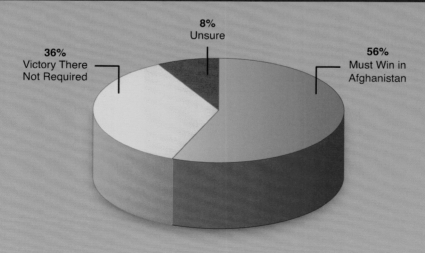

Americans Think Afghanistan Is Central to the War on Terror

The majority of Americans think America must win in Afghanistan if the broader war on terrorism is to be a success.

Question: "Do you think the United States must win the war in Afghanistan in order for the broader war on terrorism to be a success, or do you think the war on terrorism can be a success without the United States winning the war in Afghanistan?"

8%
Unsure

36%
Victory There
Not Required

56%
Must Win in
Afghanistan

Taken from: ABC News/*Washington Post* poll, December 10–13, 2009.

and need not be repeated here. It's enough to say that for the next six years, the Iraq war drew the dominant share of our troops, our resources, our diplomacy, and our national attention—and that the decision to go into Iraq caused substantial rifts between America and much of the world. . . .

Terrorists Are Returning to Afghanistan

While we've achieved hard-earned milestones in Iraq, the situation in Afghanistan has deteriorated. After escaping across the border into Pakistan in 2001 and 2002, al Qaeda's leadership established a safe haven there. Although a legitimate government was elected by the Afghan people, it's been hampered by corruption, the drug trade, an under-developed economy, and insufficient security forces.

Over the last several years, the Taliban has maintained common cause with al Qaeda, as they both seek an overthrow of the Afghan government. Gradually, the Taliban has begun to control additional swaths of territory in Afghanistan, while engaging in increasingly brazen and devastating attacks of terrorism against the Pakistani people. . . .

> **FAST FACT**
>
> According to a 2010 Quinnipiac University poll, 61 percent of Americans believe eliminating the threat from terrorists operating from Afghanistan is a worthwhile goal for American troops to fight and possibly die for.

Afghanistan is not lost, but for years it has moved backwards. There's no imminent threat of the government being overthrown, but the Taliban has gained momentum. Al Qaeda has not reemerged in Afghanistan in the same numbers as before 9/11, but they retain their safe havens along the border. And our forces lack the full support they need to effectively train and partner with Afghan security forces and better secure the population. Our new commander in Afghanistan—General McChrystal—has reported that the security situation is more serious than he anticipated. In short: The status quo is not sustainable. . . .

A Renewed Commitment to Afghanistan

As Commander-in-Chief, I have determined that it is in our vital national interest to send an additional 30,000 U.S. troops to Afghanistan. After 18 months, our troops will begin to come home. These are the resources that we need to seize the initiative, while building the Afghan capacity that can allow for a responsible transition of our forces out of Afghanistan.

I do not make this decision lightly. I opposed the war in Iraq precisely because I believe that we must exercise restraint in the use of military force, and always consider the long-term consequences of our actions. We have been at war now for eight years, at enormous cost in lives and resources. Years of debate over Iraq and terrorism have left our unity on national security issues in tatters, and created a highly polarized and partisan backdrop for this effort. And having just experienced the worst economic crisis since the Great Depression, the American people are understandably focused on rebuilding our economy and putting people to work here at home.

Most of all, I know that this decision asks even more of you—a military that, along with your families, has already borne the heaviest of all burdens. As President, I have signed a letter of condolence to the family of each American who gives their life in these wars. I have read the letters from the parents and spouses of those who deployed. I visited our courageous wounded warriors at Walter Reed [an army hospital]. I've traveled to Dover to meet the flag-draped caskets of 18 Americans returning home to their final resting place. I see firsthand the terrible wages of war. If I did not think that the security of the United States and the safety of the American people were at stake in Afghanistan, I would gladly order every single one of our troops home tomorrow.

Our Security Is at Stake

So, no, I do no make this decision lightly. I make this decision because I am convinced that our security is at stake in Afghanistan and Pakistan. This is the epicenter of violent extremism practiced by al Qaeda. It is from here that we were attacked on 9/11, and it is from here that new attacks are being plotted as I speak. This is no idle danger; no hypothetical threat. In the last few months alone, we have apprehended extremists within our borders who were sent here from the border region of Afghanistan and Pakistan to commit new acts of terror. And this danger will only grow if the region slides backwards, and al Qaeda can operate with impunity. We must keep the pressure on al Qaeda, and to do that, we must increase the stability and capacity of our partners in the region.

Of course, this burden is not ours alone to bear. This is not just America's war. Since 9/11, al Qaeda's safe havens have been the source of attacks against London and Amman [Jordan] and Bali [Indonesia]. The people and governments of both Afghanistan and Pakistan are endangered. And the stakes are even higher within a nuclear-armed Pakistan, because we know that al Qaeda and other extremists seek nuclear weapons, and we have every reason to believe that they would use them.

We Will Defeat Al Qaeda in Afghanistan

These facts compel us to act along with our friends and allies. Our overarching goal remains the same: to disrupt, dismantle, and defeat al Qaeda in Afghanistan and Pakistan, and to prevent its capacity to threaten America and our allies in the future.

To meet that goal, we will pursue the following objectives within Afghanistan. We must deny al Qaeda a safe haven. We must reverse the Taliban's momentum and deny it the ability to overthrow the government. And we must strengthen the capacity of Afghanistan's security forces and government so that they can take lead responsibility for Afghanistan's future.

EVALUATING THE AUTHORS' ARGUMENTS:

In this viewpoint Obama claims that war in Afghanistan is central to keeping Americans safe from terrorist attacks at home. How do you think Paul R. Pillar, author of the following viewpoint, would respond to this claim? Write one paragraph that summarizes each perspective. Then, state with which author you agree, and why.

Fighting the War in Afghanistan Encourages Terrorism

Paul R. Pillar

"Extension of the counterinsurgency in Afghanistan is more likely to increase than to decrease the probability that Americans inside the United States will fall victim to terrorism."

In the following viewpoint Paul R. Pillar argues that fighting in Afghanistan will not prevent terrorism and may even make terrorism worse. He explains that after the United States invaded Afghanistan in 2001, it disrupted the terrorist network there but scattered terrorists all over the globe. Pillar says such people do not need a place like Afghanistan to plot attacks— they can do that from any city anywhere in the world. Furthermore, Pillar says the war in Afghanistan has inflamed anti-American sentiment, which in turn has created and inspired even more terrorists. Pillar says America's biggest terrorist problem now stems not from people in Afghanistan but from small-scale terrorists, several of which live in the United States. Since these people are not located in Afghanistan, Pillar says fighting a war there is not going to do any-

Paul R. Pillar, "Afghanistan Is Not Making Americans Safer," *Foreign Policy in Focus,* November 19, 2009.

thing to stop them. Pillar believes that much terrorism stems from anger at the United States, and continuing the war in Afghanistan only makes that anger grow. As a result, Pillar concludes the war in Afghanistan will not reduce terrorism and may even make it worse.

Pillar is a former intelligence officer and the director of graduate studies at Georgetown University's Security Studies Program.

AS YOU READ, CONSIDER THE FOLLOWING QUESTIONS:

1. Why, according to Pillar, can fighting in Afghanistan not prevent terrorist attacks like the one perpetrated by Nidal Hasan, the Fort Hood shooter?
2. What do the Taliban have no interest in, according to Pillar?
3. Why, according to the author, have some Afghans who dislike the Taliban taken up arms *against* America?

I n the light of several incidents or alleged plots that have been in the news in recent months [2009]—the Fort Hood shootings[1] and the break-up of a terrorist ring in Colorado[2]—it is appropriate to . . . re-examine the terrorist threat to the U.S. homeland, and how the debate over troop levels in Afghanistan might affect it.

Two Ways to Think About Terrorism

The most important patterns in international terrorism, with particular reference to threats to the U.S. homeland, in the eight years since the 9/11 attacks can be summarized in two trends pointing in different directions. The first is that the group that accomplished 9/11, al Qaeda, is—although still a threat—less capable of pulling off something of that magnitude than it was in 2001. This is possible in large part because of a variety of measures that the outrage of the American public made politically possible in a way that was not possible before 9/11. These include enhanced defensive security measures at home as well as expanded offensive efforts overseas that have eroded al Qaeda's organizational infrastructure.

1. In which soldier Nidal Hasan fatally shot twelve people at a military base on November 5, 2009.
2. In which authorities apprehended people accused of plotting attacks within America.

The other major pattern or trend is that the broader violent jihadist movement of which al Qaeda is a part is probably at least as large and strong as it was eight years ago. Here again, some of our own actions have been major contributors. The war in Iraq was one such action. It provided a jihadists' training ground and networking opportunity similar to what the war against the Soviets in Afghanistan had provided two decades earlier. And in the words of the U.S. intelligence community, the war in Iraq became a *cause célèbre* for radical Islamists.

The overall result of these two trends is a terrorist threat that is more diffuse than it was several years ago. The centers of action and initiative for possible attacks, including ones against the U.S. homeland, are more numerous than they were several years ago.

An Emergence of Homegrown Terror

Against this backdrop is the specter—raised anew by some of the recent incidents—of people in the United States, including U.S. citizens, adopting some variant of radical Islamism and perpetrating terrorist attacks within the United States. The possibility is worthy of attention, if for no other reason because of the operational advantages and opportunities this represents for terrorists. Home-grown perpetrators have significant advantages over foreign operatives who, like the 9/11 terrorists, come into the country from abroad to commit their deed. The natives do not have to deal with enhanced border control procedures. They do not stand out. They are, in short, harder to detect. And they are more familiar with the territory and with their targets.

These operational advantages would make U.S. citizens or residents attractive recruiting targets for foreign terrorist groups hoping to conduct operations within the United States. But for the same operational reasons, any U.S. persons who do become terrorists would present a significant counterterrorist challenge even without having any affiliation with al Qaeda or some other foreign group.

Terrorism Has Risen Since War in Afghanistan Began

Since the war on terror began with the invasion of Afghanistan in 2001, more terrorist groups have taken up arms against the United States. Although terrorist activity by al Qaeda has gone down, there has been a significant increase in terrorist activity among al Qaeda affiliates or people inspired by al Qaeda.

Number of global neo-jihadi terrorist networks in the West

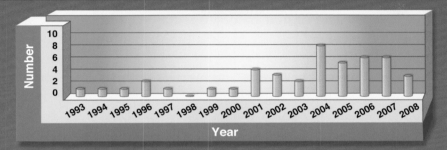

Global terrorist plots in the West

Global terrorist overseas training

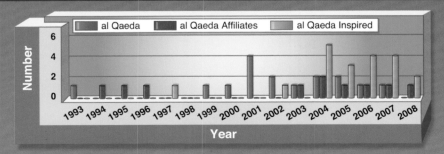

Taken from: Marc Sageman, "Confronting al Qaeda: Understanding the Threat in Afghanistan and Beyond," Testimony to the Senate Foreign Relations Committee, October 7, 2009, pp 3–4, 10.

War in Afghanistan Cannot Stop Home-Grown Terrorism

A common and reassuring observation among those who have studied the problem of home-grown terrorism is that the United States is less vulnerable than most European countries to terrorism and other political violence committed by their own Muslim populations. The reason is that American Muslims are better integrated and less ghettoized than their counterparts in Europe. But ghettoes are not a necessity, and community integration is not a foolproof safeguard, when it comes to individuals or small groups committing what still can be significant acts of violence.

Incidents to date cannot be described as yet adding up to a significant home-grown Islamist terrorist problem in the United States. But episodes like the shooting at Fort Hood suggest the possibility of more, and the sort of reasons and motivations that could make for more. And this does not depend on any recruiting successes or training activity by the likes of al Qaeda.

An Increase in Small-Scale Terrorists

The security measures implemented since 9/11 increase the importance of lone individuals or very small groups that may emerge within

Some experts say that Nidal Hasan's shooting spree at Fort Hood on April 9, 2010, is indicative of a new terrorist threat that comes from inside the United States.

the United States, relative to the importance of an established foreign terrorist organization such as al Qaeda. Those security measures have made it harder to conduct a terrorist spectacular like 9/11, where the resources, sophistication, and experience of such an organization would be most relevant. This leaves the many more mundane but less rectifiable vulnerabilities in American society. A disturbing and unavoidable fact is that just about anyone can stage a shoot-'em-up in any of countless public places in the United States. This is low-tech and unsophisticated, but it can cause enough carnage to make a significant impact on the American consciousness. The likely shape of future terrorist methods of attack in the United States is best represented by what happened at Fort Hood, or by the "D.C. sniper" episode that traumatized the national capital area a few years ago [in October 2002], an episode about which we were reminded when the principal perpetrator was executed just last week [in November 2009].

The War in Afghanistan Does Not Diminish Anti-American Sentiments

All of this has implications for the effect, if any, of our own counter-terrorist and military operations overseas on the level of threat to the U.S. homeland. Some such operations, including the firing of missiles from unmanned aircraft at individual targets in northwest Pakistan and elsewhere, have contributed to the eroding of the organizational capabilities of foreign terrorist groups and specifically al Qaeda. To the extent those capabilities are relevant to possible attacks on the U.S. homeland—and for the reasons I mentioned, that relevance is limited—they might have some positive effect on homeland security. Kinetic operations do not diminish the ideological and inspirational role that now is probably the more important contribution that al Qaeda makes to threats to American security.

The Taliban Do Not Want to Attack Americans at Home

The larger use of U.S. military force now under discussion is, of course, the counterinsurgency in Afghanistan. Pursuing and expanding that counterinsurgency would not reduce the threat of terrorist attack to the U.S. homeland. The people we are fighting—Afghans loosely grouped under the label "Taliban"—have no interest in the

United States except insofar as we are in Afghanistan and frustrating their objectives there. Their sometime allies in al Qaeda do not require a piece of physical territory to conceive, plan, prepare, and conduct terrorist operations against Western interests. To the extent the group finds a physical haven useful, even a successful counterinsurgency in line with Gen. Stanley McChrystal's strategy would still leave such havens available to the group in Pakistan, in the unsecured portions of Afghanistan, or elsewhere.

America's Presence Makes Terrorism Worse

Meanwhile the use of military force can exacerbate the terrorist threat by stoking anger against the United States and U.S. policies, largely because of the inevitable collateral damage. The anger increases the likelihood of people sympathizing with or supporting anti-U.S. terrorism, and in some cases joining or initiating such terrorism themselves. We already have seen such angry anti-Americanism in response to some of the missile strikes, and on a larger scale in response to military operations on the ground in Afghanistan, where previously dominant pro-American opinion has in large part dissipated. An expansion of the counterinsurgency would add resentment against the United States as a perceived occupying power to the anger over collateral damage.

We also have already seen such sentiments translate into anti-U.S. violence in Afghanistan in the form of many Afghans who have no liking for Taliban ideology or rule but have taken up arms to oppose American forces. Similar sentiments can have similar effects far from the field of battle, including in the U.S. homeland. Of all the elements of terrorism and counterterrorism that move easily across continents and oceans in a globalized world, emotion-stoking news about controversial policies and events is one of the easiest to move. However one chooses to characterize what Maj. Nidal Hasan did at Fort Hood, his reported sentiments about America's current overseas wars and how these sentiments figured into the action he took illustrate a phenomenon that we should not be surprised to see more of, albeit in different forms.

The War Increases the Risk of Terrorism

The indirect effects of anger and resentment are inherently more difficult to gauge or even to perceive than the direct effects of military action in seizing or securing territory or in killing individual operatives. But this does not mean they are less important in affecting terrorist threats. They are the main reason that in my judgment, expansion and extension of the counterinsurgency in Afghanistan is more likely to increase than to decrease the probability that Americans inside the United States will fall victim to terrorism in the years ahead.

EVALUATING THE AUTHOR'S ARGUMENTS:

In this viewpoint Paul R. Pillar uses history, facts, examples, and appeals to reason to make his argument that the war in Afghanistan cannot reduce terrorism. He does not, however, use any quotations to support his point. If you were to rewrite this article and insert quotations, what authorities might you quote from? Where would you place these quotations to bolster the points Pillar makes?

Viewpoint

3

Stopping Rogue Nations from Obtaining Weapons of Mass Destruction Can Prevent Terrorism

"No nation today has as extensive a record of supporting terrorism as Iran."

Steven Emerson and Joel Himelfarb

In the following viewpoint Steven Emerson and Joel Himelfarb argue that rogue nations like Iran are likely to arm terrorists. They document links between Iran and the terrorist groups al Qaeda and Hezbollah, saying that terrorists from both groups have trained in Iran and negotiated with Iran for weapons. Emerson and Himelfarb contend that contrary to popular opinion, Iran would have no qualms about arming terrorist groups with nuclear weaponry. They say Iran has already been caught supplying Hezbollah terrorists with weapons to use

Steven Emerson and Joel Himelfarb, "Would Iran Provide a Nuclear Weapon to Terrorists?" *inFocus Quarterly,* Winter, 2009. Reproduced by permission.

in attacks against Israel. The authors see nothing to stop Iran from using these same smuggling routes to get nuclear and other weapons of mass destruction to terrorists. For all these reasons, Emerson and Himelfarb conclude that preventing Iran from obtaining weapons of mass destruction can significantly reduce the threat from terrorists.

Emerson is the executive director of the Investigative Project on Terrorism (IPT) where Himelfarb is a senior writer.

AS YOU READ, CONSIDER THE FOLLOWING QUESTIONS:
1. Who is Ali Mohammed, and how do the authors factor him into their argument?
2. What al Qaeda chief of military operations do the authors say was trained at Hezbollah facilities?
3. What weapons were seized from the MV Francop, according to Emerson and Himelfarb?

The United States seeks to negotiate an end to Iran's bid for nuclear weapons. U.S. and European officials have laid out scenarios whereby Iran could potentially threaten the surrounding Arab states, Israel, or even Europe with missiles equipped with nuclear warheads. But there is strikingly little discussion among policymakers about the possibility Iran might share nuclear weapons with one of the many terrorist organizations it supports.

When this worst-case scenario is raised, analysts usually focus on Hezbollah, the Lebanese Shi'ite terrorist group founded in the early 1980s by Iran's Revolutionary Guards. However, al-Qaeda has a far more extensive history of seeking to acquire these weapons, and as the *9/11 Report* stated, Osama bin Laden's network retains nominal yet murky ties with Iran. Despite a history of distrust and feuding between Shiite and Sunni Muslims, Tehran and al-Qaeda share common enemies in the United States and Israel. This has yielded cooperation in recent years.

Al-Qaeda and Iran Are Linked

Former Assistant U.S. Attorney Andrew McCarthy, who prosecuted some of the major U.S. terror cases of the 1990s, outlined in detail in

National Review Online the cooperation between Iran and al-Qaeda. McCarthy points to the case of Ali Mohammed, a shadowy Egyptian who eventually immigrated to the United States and served in the U.S. Army. Unbeknownst to U.S. intelligence, Mohammed was also a senior al-Qaeda trainer and served as bin Laden's personal bodyguard. At bin Laden's direction, Mohammed conducted surveillance of various potential bombing targets including the U.S. Embassy in Nairobi, Kenya.

When he pled guilty in 2000 to participating in al-Qaeda's war against the United States, Mohammed cited the existence of "contacts between al-Qaeda and al-Jihad organization [Egyptian Islamic Jihad, headed by Zawahiri], on one side, and Iran and Hezbollah on the other side. I arranged security for a meeting in the Sudan between [Imad Mugniyeh], Hezbollah's chief, and bin Laden."

Mohammed further stated that Hezbollah provided explosives training for al-Qaeda and al-Jihad. Iran, in turn, supplied al-Jihad with weapons. Iran also used Hezbollah to "supply explosives disguised to look like rocks."

Al-Qaeda Terrorists Have Trained in Iran

Mohammed's disclosure should not have come as a surprise. When the U.S. indicted bin Laden in 1998, the Justice Department charged that he had called for al-Qaeda to "put aside its differences with Shi'ite Muslim terrorist organizations, including the government of Iran and its affiliated terrorist group Hezbollah, to cooperate against the perceived common enemy, the United States and its allies."

The indictment added, "Al-Qaeda also forged alliances . . . with the government of Iran and its associated terrorist group Hezbollah for the purpose of working together against their perceived common enemies in the West, particularly the United States."

When it released its final report in 2004, the 9/11 Commission noted that, "senior al Qaeda operatives and trainers traveled to Iran to receive training in explosives. In the fall of 1993, another such delegation went to the Bekaa Valley in Lebanon for further training in explosives as well as intelligence and security."

That instruction at Hezbollah facilities included al-Qaeda's top military committee members. One of those who received training from Hezbollah, McCarthy noted, was Saif al-Adel, al-Qaeda's chief of military operations and a "driving force" behind the 1998 Africa embassy bombings. He was also tied to the U.S.S. *Cole* bombing in 2000, and was believed to have trained some of the September 11 hijackers. . . .

Do Not Doubt Iran Could Give WMDs to Terrorists

Terrorism analysts in Washington need to be asking: Under what circumstances might Iran decide to up the ante and transfer WMD [weapons of mass destruction] technology to terrorist organizations?

Diplomats typically dismiss the possibility. They acknowledge that this would be a terrible thing, but express doubt that Iran would take such a drastic step for two reasons.

First, they argue that Tehran itself is uncomfortable at the prospect of terrorists acquiring such weapons. Second, they argue that the Iranian leadership understands that if a nuclear weapon is transferred to al-Qaeda and used to attack the United States or any of its allies, the retaliation would be overwhelming.

To be sure, analysts should not underestimate the importance of American power as a deterrent. But it is equally important to understand that, with Iran, deterrence has its limits. No nation today has as extensive a record of supporting terrorism as Iran, and Western policies in place until now have utterly failed to deter Iran from facilitating terrorism using conventional weapons.

> **FAST FACT**
>
> According to the International Institute for Strategic Studies, Iran—a known supporter of terrorism—could have enough enriched uranium to build a nuclear bomb by the end of 2010.

U.S. deterrence has been eroded by Iran's perception of American weakness, and by the fact that the Iranian regime has been able to foment terrorism and violence against the United States and the West for more than 30 years and get away with it. Deterrence is further weakened by the instability of Iranian President Mahmoud Ahmadinejad, who seems not to fear conflict with the West.

Iran Could Give Nukes to Hezbollah Terrorists

Iran could also provide a nuclear weapon to any of its proxy terrorist organizations in conflict with Israel. Indeed, Iran could see this as an insurance policy. In the event that Israel launches a preemptive attack on Iranian nuclear facilities, Tehran may conclude that it has nothing to lose by turning nuclear technology over to terrorists—notably Hezbollah.

Iran already has smuggling routes to the group. Recently, it smuggled massive quantities of weapons to Hezbollah in Lebanon, in an attempt to help it to rebuild the weapons arsenal destroyed by Israel during the 2006 war. As a result of that smuggling, Hezbollah now has more than three times the number of missiles it had at the start of that war. Israeli military officials acknowledged in November that Hezbollah now has Iranian-made Fajr rockets that reach Tel Aviv and possibly Israel's nuclear facility at Dimona.

The Israelis are doing their best to stop the flow of weapons. On November 3, Israeli commandos intercepted an arms shipment on its way from Iran to Hezbollah. The weapons were transported aboard the MV *Francop*, a cargo ship flying the Antiguan flag. Hidden aboard the civilian vessel were three-dozen shipping containers holding weaponry for Hezbollah. At 500 tons, the *Francop* was carrying a quantity of armaments at least 10 times as large as that aboard the *Karine-A*, a ship that Iran loaded up with 50 tons of advanced weaponry for Yasser Arafat's Palestinian Authority in Gaza. It was captured by Israel in January 2002.

Iran Has Smuggled Weapons to Terrorists Before

In the *Francop* case, the weapons seized aboard the ship included 3,000 recoilless gun shells, 9,000 mortar bombs, and more than half a million rounds of small-arms ammunition. Also found aboard the ship were 2,800 rockets. English- and Farsi-language markings on the polyethylene sacks containing the munitions proved that Iran's National Petrochemical Company produced the sacks.

In January 2009, Cypriot authorities captured a shipment of anti-tank weapons, artillery and rocket-manufacturing materials for manufacturing rockets on a Cypriot ship leased by an Iranian firm. Intelligence officials believe the weaponry was bound for Hezbollah forces in Lebanon.

In May 2007, the Kurdish PKK terror group derailed an Iranian train in southeastern Turkey carrying rocket launchers, mortar shells, and light arms to Syria (possibly destined for Hezbollah.) In December 2003 and January 2004, after humanitarian assistance was flown into southern Iran for earthquake victims, the Iranian Revolutionary Guards used the return flights to Damascus to smuggle arms to Hezbollah.

A Nuclear World

Though Iran does not yet have nuclear weapons, experts fear they are on their way to developing them—and might share the technology with terrorists. Experts also worry terrorists might steal or buy nuclear weapons from North Korea, Pakistan, or from unsecured Russian stockpiles.

Nuclear Warheads

Number of warheads, 2009	Country								
	Russia	U.S.	France	Israel	UK	China	Pakistan	India	North Korea
Intercontinental missiles	1,355	550	-	-	-	121	-	-	-
Short-range missiles	576	1,152	-	-	-	-	-	-	-
Bombs	856	500	60	-	-	55	-	-	-
Submarines/ non-strategic	2,050	500	240	-	192	-	-	-	-
In reserve/ awaiting dismantlement	8,150	6,700	-	-	-	-	-	-	-
Total Now	12,987	9,552	300	200	192	176	90	75	2
Total in 2000	21,000	10,577	350	0	185	400	0	0	0

Taken from: "The World in Active Nuclear Weapons," *Guardian*, April 6, 2009, and Bulletin of the Atomic Scientists.

These are the instances in which weapons were captured. There are untold numbers of Iranian shipments that get through. The question that analysts must now answer is: could a nuclear weapon get through, too? . . .

The Iranian Nuclear Threat

The dangers of an Iranian nuclear weapon are many. While the dangers of the conventional missile threat have been made clear, the danger of an Iranian bomb in the hands of terrorist organizations requires further analysis. The free world dismisses such threats at its own peril.

EVALUATING THE AUTHORS' ARGUMENTS:

The authors of this viewpoint and Daniel Byman, author of the following viewpoint, all agree that Iran has transferred conventional weapons to terrorists. But they disagree on whether Iran would give nuclear weapons to terrorists. After reading both viewpoints, with which one do you agree? Why? List at least three pieces of evidence that helped you form your opinion.

Rogue Nations Are Not Likely to Give Weapons of Mass Destruction to Terrorists

Daniel Byman

"Iran's past behavior suggests it is not likely to provide chemical, biological, radiological, or nuclear weapons to a terrorist group."

In the following viewpoint Daniel Byman argues that a rogue nation like Iran is unlikely to supply terrorists with weapons of mass destruction (WMDs). Byman concedes that Iran is a supporter of terrorism. However, he says, Iran has scaled back its support of terrorism in significant ways since the 1990s. Although it supports some terrorist groups, Byman says it would probably not give WMDs to such groups because such a move would threaten its own safety. Terrorists are loyal to no nation, and Iran might rightly fear terrorists would use the weapons to attack it. Iran also would not want to risk the threat of retaliation from the United States should it catch terrorists using Iran-supplied WMDs. Byman points out that Iran has had biological and chemical weapons for years and has never given them to terrorists—in his opinion, there is no reason to think it would start now or that it would offer terrorists nuclear weapons should it become able to develop them. For all of these reasons, Byman concludes that Iran is unlikely to give weapons of mass destruction to terrorists.

Byman is assistant professor in the Security Studies Program at Georgetown University and a nonresident senior fellow at the Saban Center for Middle East Policy.

AS YOU READ, CONSIDER THE FOLLOWING QUESTIONS:

1. Why did Iran dramatically cut back on terrorist operations in Europe and the Gulf states, according to Byman?
2. Why does Byman say Iran stopped supporting terrorist attacks on U.S. forces after the 1996 Khobar Towers bombing?
3. What "truly grave event" does Byman say might cause Iran to give WMDs to terrorists?

Since the Islamic Revolution in 1979 [when Iran's monarchy under the Shah was overthrown], Iran has been one of the world's most active sponsors of terrorism. Tehran has armed, trained, financed, inspired, organized, and otherwise supported dozens of violent groups over the years. Iran has backed not only groups in its Persian Gulf neighborhood, but also terrorists and radicals in Lebanon, the Palestinian territories, Bosnia, the Philippines, and elsewhere. This support remains strong even today: the U.S. government regularly contends that Iran is tied to an array of radical groups in Iraq.

Yet despite Iran's very real support for terrorism for more than the last 25 years and its possession of chemical weapons for over 15 years, Tehran has not transferred unconventional systems to terrorists. Iran is likely to continue this restraint and not transfer chemical, biological, or nuclear weapons for several reasons. First, providing terrorists with such unconventional weapons offers Iran few tactical advantages as these groups are able to operate effectively with existing methods and weapons. Second, Iran has become more cautious in its backing of terrorists in recent years. And third, it is highly aware that any major escalation in its support for terrorism would incur U.S. wrath and international condemnation. . . .

Iran Has Cut Support for Terrorism

Iran's use of terrorism has changed dramatically since the 1980s. Most importantly from a U.S. point of view, Iran appears not to target Americans directly, although it still retains the capability to do so and in Iraq some groups with links to Iran have fought with coalition forces. Iran instead uses terrorism as a form of deterrence, "casing" U.S. embassies and other facilities to give it a response should the United States step up pressure. Tehran also dramatically cut back on operations in Europe and the Gulf states since the early 1990s. Iranian officials feared that attacks on Iranian dissidents there would lead to European support for sanctions and reduce investment in Iran's economy. In the mid-1990s, Iran's then President Ali Akbar Hashemi Rafsanjani engineered a rapprochement with the Arabian Gulf states, which led Iran to stop actively trying to overthrow those regimes, though it retains ties to a number of Shi'a groups there. Taken together, these three shifts represent a dramatic change in Iran's support for terrorism.

Today, Iran uses terrorism and support for radicals in several distinct ways. Particularly important for the United States are Tehran's close relationship with the Lebanese [political and paramilitary group] Hizballah; support for anti-Israel Palestinian groups; ties to various factions within Iraq; and loose contacts with Al Qaeda. . . .

> **FAST FACT**
>
> When one hundred foreign policy experts were asked in 2007 which nation they thought would be most likely to transfer nuclear materials to terrorists, 74 percent said Pakistan—an ally of the United States.

Iran Has Shown Restraint with Terrorists

Although Iran's support for terrorists groups have made them more lethal (particularly with regard to Hizballah), Tehran is also a source of

Iran Unlikely to Give WMDs to Terrorists

Each year, *Foreign Policy* and the Center for American Progress poll one hundred top foreign policy experts on what they think of trends in terrorism. Each year more of these experts say it is less likely Iran would transfer nuclear weapons to terrorists.

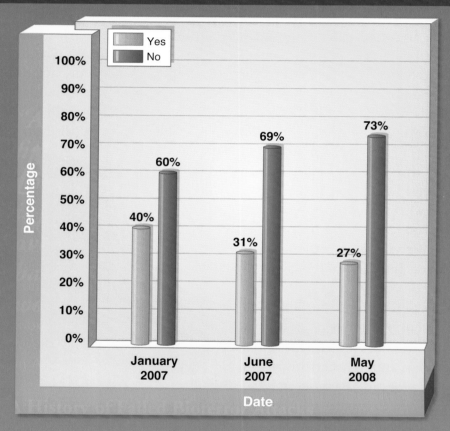

Question: "Is it likely that Iran would transfer nuclear weapons to terrorists?"

Taken from: The Terrorism Index, *Foreign Policy*, September–October 2008, p. 82.

restraint on its proxies. Most importantly, Tehran takes seriously the threat of escalation from Israel, the United States, or other potential victims should its proxies wreak massive violence. Iran stopped supporting attacks by Gulf Shi'a [Muslims] on U.S. forces in the Persian

Gulf after the 1996 Khobar Towers bombing—despite a continued desire to expel Americans from the region—in part because it feared an increase in political, economic, and perhaps even military pressure. After the bombing, Iranian leaders worried they might have crossed the line they had long walked between confrontation and provocation. Similarly, Iran did not let the SCIRI [the Supreme Assembly for the Islamic Revolution in Iraq] make an all-out push to topple Saddam [Hussein's] regime when it was reeling after the 1991 Gulf War—despite the massacres of Iraqi Shi'a—because Tehran feared a confrontation with the victorious U.S. and other coalition forces.

The restraints states impose are often best observed in what terrorist groups do not do. As Iran sought to improve its reputation in Europe and the Middle East, the Lebanese Hizballah curtailed its attacks on targets in Europe and on Israeli targets worldwide, focusing instead on expelling Israel from the security zone along the Lebanon-Israel border: a struggle widely seen as legitimate in many parts of the world. . . .

Iran Is Unlikely to Give WMDs to Terrorists

The picture painted thus far is not pretty, but it is not hopeless either. One bright spot is that Iran's past behavior suggests it is not likely to provide chemical, biological, radiological, or nuclear weapons to a terrorist group. Because these weapons can be devastating—or, at the very least, psychologically terrifying even when the number directly affected is low—they are far more likely to provoke escalation. In addition, these weapons are widely seen as heinous, potentially de-legitimating both the group and its state sponsor. Perhaps not surprisingly, Iran has not transferred chemical or biological weapons or agents to its proxies, despite its capability to do so.

Tehran has also sought at least a degree of deniability in its use of terrorism—a reason it often works through the Lebanese Hizballah to this day when backing terrorists. As Iran expert Kenneth Pollack notes, a chemical or biological attack (to say nothing of a nuclear strike) would lead the victim to respond with full force almost immediately. The use of proxies or cutouts would not shield Iran from retaliation.

Deterred by the Threat from the United States

September 11 has also had a limiting effect. The attacks occurred over a year after the Israeli withdrawal from Lebanon. The tremendous worldwide concern about terrorism, and the active U.S. campaign against Al Qaeda, made Iran's proxies cautious about any attacks that would lead them to be compared to Al Qaeda.

Nor do Iran's favored proxies actively seek weapons of mass destruction as does Al Qaeda. They appear to recognize the "red line" drawn by the United States and other powers with regard to terrorist use of these weapons. Moreover, their current tactics and systems enable them to inflict considerable casualties. Indeed, some of the more available types of chemical and biological agents would be difficult for even a skilled terrorist group to use to inflict mass casualties, although the psychological impact would be considerable from even a limited attack with unconventional weapons.

Tehran is not likely to change its behavior on this score except in the most extreme circumstances. Traditional terrorist tactics such as assassinations and truck bombs have proven effective for Tehran. Only in the event of a truly grave threat such as an invasion of Iran would many of Tehran's traditional cautions go out the window.

EVALUATING THE AUTHORS' ARGUMENTS:

Byman claims one reason Iran is unlikely to give WMDs to terrorists is because it fears retaliation from the United States. How do Emerson and Himelfarb, authors of the previous viewpoint, refute this claim? Summarize each perspective, and then state with which one you agree.

The United States Can Prevent Terrorism by Winning Hearts and Minds

Michael Chertoff

"*To prevent the growth of terrorist groups themselves, the United States must pursue strategies to win nations and peoples to its side.*"

Michael Chertoff served as secretary of Homeland Security from 2005 to 2009. In the following viewpoint he argues that the United States can prevent terrorism by quelling anti-Americanism. He explains that although the U.S. military has successfully fought terrorists in places like Iraq and Afghanistan, the military is the wrong long-term solution to the problem. Chertoff says it is not enough to stop people who are already terrorists—a longer-lasting solution is to prevent people from hating America in the first place. To do that, he recommends the United States offer humanitarian aid in countries where anti-American groups recruit terrorists. He says helping after natural disasters, building schools, and other virtuous activities will encourage people to see the United States as a benevolent nation and be less likely to want to attack it. Chertoff concludes that fostering good will toward the United States is the best way to permanently solve the problem of terrorism.

AS YOU READ, CONSIDER THE FOLLOWING QUESTIONS:

1. In the context of this viewpoint, what does the author mean by the term "soft power"?
2. What does Chertoff say are the two major factors driving the growth of modern terrorism?
3. According to the author, what were the findings of polls conducted by the group Terror-Free Tomorrow?

Since its establishment five years ago, the Department of Homeland Security has played a pivotal role in mobilizing the efforts of the United States government to prevent and deter terrorists and other dangerous people from attacking the country. These efforts have yielded positive results: By any fair measure, the United States is safer and more secure today. Yet it would be a mistake to conclude that the threat posed by terrorism has entirely disappeared or has ceased to be of critical concern. In the words of the July 2007 National Intelligence Estimate, "we face a persistent and evolving terrorist threat over the next three years." In [the Islamist terrorist group] al Qaeda and like-minded organizations, the United States and its allies confront a relentless and resourceful adversary rooted in a violent, extremist ideology. Its adherents continue to wage war against civilization, including mainstream Muslims, while seeking to harness further the power of modern technology and globalization to achieve dominance and far greater destructive capabilities in the future.

Consequently, it is imperative that over the next decade, the United States, in concert with its friends and allies, retain every option at its disposal and apply every available tool or strategy where appropriate against this threat. Certainly that includes the effective use of military options when necessary as well as other tools that may reduce the ability of terrorists to carry out attacks. Most importantly, however, in order to prevent the growth of terrorist groups themselves, the United States must pursue strategies to win nations and peoples to its side. Use of such "soft power"—a term coined by Harvard University professor Joseph Nye—can help the United States and its allies reduce the appeal of terrorist organizations and deter individuals from joining them.

America's relief efforts in the aftermath of the 2004 Indonesian tsunami significantly changed America's favorability rating among Muslims of the region.

We Must Keep People from Becoming Terrorists

The use of military action in recent years against the terrorists has included deposing the Taliban [a Sunni Islamist political group] in Afghanistan and combating al Qaeda in Iraq. During this time, the United States and its allies have also acted to frustrate three key enablers of terrorism—communications, finance, and travel. They continue to intercept and disrupt communications and actively work to freeze the assets of groups and individuals that support terrorism. When it comes to travel, the United States employs three key strategies: collecting limited bits of commercial information in order to identify travelers warranting closer scrutiny, screening incoming individuals through biometrics, and building a system of secure travel documentation through the Western Hemisphere Travel Initiative.

> **FAST FACT**
>
> A 2009 ABC News poll of Iraqi citizens found that 56 percent approved of the 2003 invasion of their country; 65 percent say their life is better than it was in years past; and 64 percent want to see democracy thrive in their country.

Taken together, these measures constitute a layered approach: deterring terrorists from entering the United States, capturing or killing them before they embark on the journey, and stopping them during their travel.

Unfortunately, such measures, while necessary, will likely leave us short of a lasting victory in the safeguarding of the country. To prevail, we must not only work hard to prevent terrorists from attacking, but we must also expend equal effort to prevent people from becoming terrorists in the first place. That requires addressing the two major factors that are driving the growth of terrorism in the 21st century: the continued presence of failed political and economic systems in parts of the developing world, and the emergence of violent Islamic extremism as the most visible competing ideology for those mired in that dismal status quo.

Fighting the Ideology of Extension

Given these two factors, the course ahead should be clear. The United States must fight not only the extremists, but the ideology of their extremism. It must stand firmly against malignant ideas which can only cause further poverty, degradation, and hopelessness by turning the clock back centuries. It must offer the alternative ideals of liberty and democracy, ideals which have brought more progress to more people over the past few centuries than in all the prior centuries combined. In other words, as during the Cold War, the situation must be seen as a

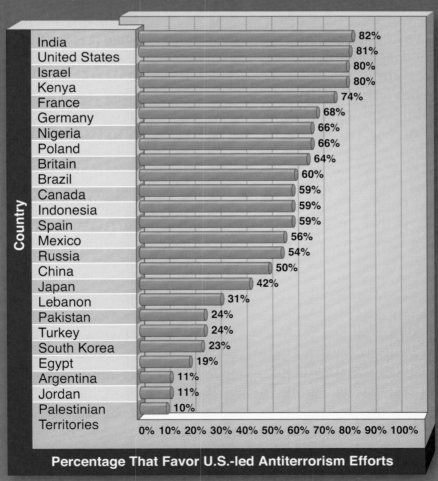

United States Antiterrorism Efforts

In 2009, more countries approved of U.S.-led antiterrorism efforts than in any other year since 2002. Some believe approval—or winning the hearts and minds—of people across the globe is the key to overcoming terrorism.

Country	Percentage
India	82%
United States	81%
Israel	80%
Kenya	80%
France	74%
Germany	68%
Nigeria	66%
Poland	66%
Britain	64%
Brazil	60%
Canada	59%
Indonesia	59%
Spain	59%
Mexico	56%
Russia	54%
China	50%
Japan	42%
Lebanon	31%
Pakistan	24%
Turkey	24%
South Korea	23%
Egypt	19%
Argentina	11%
Jordan	11%
Palestinian Territories	10%

0% 10% 20% 30% 40% 50% 60% 70% 80% 90% 100%

Percentage That Favor U.S.-led Antiterrorism Efforts

Taken from: Pew Global Attitudes Project, 2009.

war against an ideology, a contest of ideas, and a battle for the allegiance of men and women around the world. It is not a struggle that we began; it is, however, one that we must win. The security of the United States and the world depends on it.

To stand on the sidelines would be to allow this extremist ideology to win by default. So what must we do to counter it? When proposing an alternative to radical ideology, the use of soft power becomes key. Part of this effort must involve providing immediate humanitarian aid to those who need it the most.

Using Aid to Fight Terror

This is not an unfamiliar task for the United States; the nation has been doing this throughout its history. In December 2004, for example, the United States responded to the series of catastrophic tsunamis that killed more than 225,000 people in Indonesia, India, Thailand, and Sri Lanka. The government acted immediately by committing US$350 million in relief funding to meet a wide array of human needs, ranging from food and water and health and sanitation assistance to education and cash-for-work programs. It sent 16,000 sailors and airmen to evacuate the injured and deliver aid to hundreds of thousands of people in the affected countries. According to the Center on Philanthropy at Indiana University, US private tsunami donations—cash and in-kind—exceeded US$1.8 billion.

The overwhelming majority of casualties occurred in Indonesia, the world's most populous Muslim country. While Indonesia is a democracy, the forces of Islamist extremism have been trying to gain a foothold, making it an important ideological battleground. In the wake of the tsunami, the reaction of Indonesians to US aid is instructive. Polls conducted by Terror-Free Tomorrow, a non-profit, non-partisan organization, indicate that 65 percent of Indonesians now harbor attitudes that are "more favorable" to the United States than before its response to the tsunami, with the highest percentage occurring among people under 30. A separate poll conducted by the Pew Global Attitudes Project in Indonesia reports that nearly 80 percent of Indonesians affirm that the donations gave them a more positive view of the United States.

It is also worth noting that at the same time the United States was extending its hand to Indonesia, its people were turning decisively against the al Qaeda–allied extremists responsible for the horrific bombings in Bali in 2002 and in Jakarta in 2003 and 2004. As a result, according to the Pew Research Center, support for Osama Bin Laden plummeted and has yet to recover. In 2002, nearly 60 percent of Indonesians supported him. By 2006, only 33 percent had favorable views of al Qaeda's leader.

We Must Encourage Greater Good Will Toward the United States

Indonesia is but one example of how soft power in the form of practical compassion can influence attitudes and cast this nation in a favorable light compared to its enemies. There can be little doubt that other actions, such as President George W. Bush's US$1.2 billion initiative against malaria, and his US$15 billion initial commitment to fight HIV/AIDS, have sown good seeds in areas like sub-Sahara Africa. This is yet another region where radical Islamists are attempting to capitalize on disaffection with the status quo.

More obvious examples of the potential effectiveness of foreign aid are Iraq and Afghanistan, as well as Pakistan and Lebanon. In Iraq, as in Indonesia, the extremists' reign of terror has turned many of their supporters against al Qaeda and its affiliates. Even many of the Sunnis in Iraq now back the surge, and its continued successes have led to further support for our actions. This virtuous cycle is being strengthened by developmental and reconstruction efforts. From business development to local governance, from literacy campaigns to bank reform, from rural development to school construction, the United States is quietly laying the foundation for lasting progress. Iraq remains a volatile place, but this continued work on the ground, especially when contrasted with al Qaeda's atrocities, can only produce greater good will toward the United States.

> **EVALUATING THE AUTHOR'S ARGUMENTS:**
>
> Chertoff argues that encouraging foreigners to see America as a kind, generous, and benevolent nation will keep people from wanting to become terrorists. Do you agree? Is winning hearts and minds the best strategy for combating terrorism? Or do you think a military campaign offers the best solution to terrorism? Explain your reasoning.

Preventing Radicalism in Immigrant Communities Can Prevent Terrorism

Lorenzo Vidino

"While the overwhelming majority of the American Muslim community abhors terrorism, a small segment is not impermeable to radicalization."

In the following viewpoint Lorenzo Vidino explains that terrorists often spring from immigrant communities in which people feel disenfranchised and cut off from society. Therefore, he recommends engaging and empowering members of these communities in order to prevent terrorism. Vidino describes several terrorist attacks that have been plotted by American Muslim immigrants. In his opinion, these men became "radicalized," or filled with hatred for their host country, because the United States has not done enough to incorporate them into society in a way that has bettered their lives. Vidino says military solutions will not achieve a long-term solution to terrorism because military attacks cannot keep people from wanting to become terrorists in the

Lorenzo Vidino, "Keeping a Lid on Homegrown Terrorism," *The Boston Globe,* October 5, 2009. Reproduced by permission of the author.

first place. He recommends that the United States make efforts to positively engage its immigrant Muslim communities so they will be less vulnerable to radicalization.

Vidino is a fellow at the Belfer Center for Science and International Affairs at Harvard University and a peace scholar at the United States Institute of Peace.

AS YOU READ, CONSIDER THE FOLLOWING QUESTIONS:
1. According to the author, what was the conclusion of a 2007 report by the New York Police Department? What bearing does this have on Vidino's argument?
2. What public institution does Vidino say is a potential breeding ground for radicalism?
3. In the context of this viewpoint, what does the author mean by the phrase "war of ideas"?

Terrorism dramatically regained the headlines recently [2009], as US authorities revealed the details of three unrelated plots they foiled.

Authorities in Illinois arrested Michael Finton, a 29-year-old convert to Islam in an alleged plot to blow up a federal building in Springfield. The next day a 19-year-old Jordanian national was arrested for allegedly hatching a similar plot against a Dallas skyscraper. Finally, in what has been called by authorities the most serious attempt to strike the US homeland since the Sept. 11, 2001, attacks, authorities indicted Najibullah Zazi, a longtime US resident of Afghan descent who had allegedly planned to carry out bombings with chemicals he had purchased in beauty supply stores. These events seem to confirm what authorities have been saying for the last few years: while the overwhelming majority of the American Muslim community abhors terrorism, a small segment is not impermeable to radicalization.

Fertile Soil for Radical Ideas

European authorities have long struggled with the same issue, as hundreds of European Muslims have been involved in terrorist activities.

Members of accused bomber Michael Finton's mosque meet with the press to strongly condemn his actions.

Over the last few years US authorities have questioned whether the emergence of large numbers of radicalized Muslims could also take place here.

Of course, there are differences between the United States and Europe. The first is related to the significantly better economic conditions of American Muslims. While European Muslims generally languish at the bottom of most rankings that measure economic integration, American Muslims fare significantly better. Although economic integration is not always an antidote to radicalization, it is undeniable that radical ideas find a fertile environment among unemployed and disenfranchised youth.

Geographic dispersion, immigration patterns, and tougher immigration policies have also prevented the formation of extensive recruiting and propaganda networks as those that have sprung up in Europe.

Finally, there is the fact that large segments of the American Muslim population belong to ethnicities that have traditionally espoused moderate interpretations of Islam.

While all these characteristics still hold true, they no longer represent a guarantee. A 2007 report by the New York Police Department stated that "despite the economic opportunities in the United States, the powerful gravitational pull of individuals' religious roots and identity sometimes supersede the assimilating nature of American society."

No Guarantee Against Radicalization

Factors such as perception of discrimination and frustration at US foreign policies could lead to radicalization, irrespective of favorable economic conditions. Recent cases have also shown that radicalization can touch communities where extremism is rare, such as the Albanian and the Iranian American.

Moreover, the fact that no organized group has an extensive network in the country is no longer a guarantee that radicalization cannot reach America's shores, as the Internet has replaced the need to have operatives physically spreading the propaganda on the ground. A search of jihadist [those waging a holy war on behalf of Islam] chat rooms and even of subgroups in "benign" social network sites reveal the presence of many American-born youngsters who glorify Al Qaeda's ideology.

> **FAST FACT**
>
> The accused perpetrators of several 2009 terror plots came from immigrant communities in the United States. For example, Afghan-born Najibullah Zazi, legal resident of the United States, was arrested in September 2009 for plotting a terror attack in New York. Similarly, Brooklyn-born Betim Kaziu was arrested for attempting to conspire with al Qaeda, as was Michael Finton of Illinois, for plotting to bomb a federal courthouse.

In response, aggressive counterterrorism tactics and improved intelligence sharing have allowed US authorities to dismantle cells and keep the country safe. At the same time, though, the United States seems to be lacking a long-term strategy to confront the threat. Authorities have been unable to conceive a policy that would preemptively tackle the issue of radicalization, preventing young American Muslims from embracing extremist ideas in the first place.

"Terrorism Graduates," cartoon by David Fitzsimmons, *The Arizona Star,* November 28, 2008, PoliticalCartoons .com. Copyright © 2008 David Fitzsimmons, *The Arizona Star,* and PoliticalCartoons.com. All rights reserved.

Long-Term Strategy

Various intelligence and law enforcement agencies have reached out to the academic community to better understand the social, political, and psychological causes of radicalization. But the limited understanding of the issue, coupled with the overlap of jurisdiction between often competing federal, state, and local authorities, has prevented the implementation of a systematic, nationwide program to combat radicalization.

Keeping in mind that there is no silver bullet that can stop all individuals from embracing radical ideas or violence, there are measures that the United States can adopt. Several cases have shown, for example, that prisons are a potential breeding ground for radicalism, a place where a well organized supply (radical inmates or imams) meets a large demand (disenfranchised and angry men). While respecting the inmates' religious rights, authorities must make sure that radicalization does not spread in American prisons.

The Internet is another weak spot. Policing the Web is obviously impossible, but authorities in various Muslim countries have begun infiltrating known jihadist chat rooms in order to undermine their radical views and influence their less-hardened visitors. This sort of involvement in key battlefields of the so-called war of ideas is sorely lacking in this country.

Counterterrorism Is Not Enough

Solutions are exceptionally hard to find. Europeans have long struggled with the same issue and are only now attempting to put in place coherent programs to fight radicalization, the success of which is still to be verified. Equally challenging have been efforts, on both sides of the Atlantic, to find reliable and representative organizations within various Muslim communities to be employed as partners in anti-radicalization activities.

But recent events clearly show that the issue needs to be addressed in America. Even the most aggressive counterterrorism tactics cannot stop all acts of violence. Therefore, the United States needs to make long-term plans to stem the ideas that lead people to resort to terrorism in the first place.

EVALUATING THE AUTHOR'S ARGUMENTS:

Vidino suggests the United States implement a systematic, nationwide program to combat radicalization in immigrant Muslim communities. If you were asked to help design this program, what recommendations would you make? Come up with at least three suggestions for reducing anti-Americanism and radicalization in America's immigrant communities.

Terrorism Can Be Prevented by Abandoning the War on Terror

"Abandon the notion of a 'war on terrorism.' Drop it. . . . Acknowledge that there never can be a war against terrorism because terrorism is a tactic."

Michael Lerner

Terrorism cannot be fought with war argues Michael Lerner in the following viewpoint. He explains that terrorism is a tactic, an action or technique capable of being used by countless people anywhere in the world. As such, war is the wrong response to the problem of terrorism because a military needs a formal enemy in a fixed location to fight against. A more appropriate response, says Lerner, is to treat terrorists like organized criminals and send an international police force after them. This police force would track and capture terrorists the way they would any other type of criminal. Lerner says it is unrealistic to expect that terrorism can ever be completely eradicated—however, he says it is possible to reduce the sentiments that cause people to become terrorists in the first place. Lerner concludes the

Michael Lerner, "Just Say 'No' to the War in Afghanistan," *Tikkun,* November–December, 2009. Copyright © 2009 Institute for Labor and Mental Health. Reproduced by permission of *Tikkun: A Bimonthly Jewish Critique of Politics, Culture & Society.*

United States should abandon the war on terror because not only is it the wrong format for fighting terrorists, but it actually encourages more people to take up the terrorists' cause.

Lerner is a rabbi and the editor of *Tikkun*, a progressive Jewish and interfaith magazine where this viewpoint was originally published.

AS YOU READ, CONSIDER THE FOLLOWING QUESTIONS:
1. What does Lerner say is the only way to absolutely control terrorism everywhere on the planet?
2. Why would eliminating the world's nuclear weapons help prevent terrorism, in Lerner's opinion?
3. What is Lerner's idea for a Domestic and Global Marshall Plan? What are its features and how does Lerner say it can prevent terrorism?

I t's not that it is impossible to imagine terrorists acquiring a nuclear weapon and detonating it in the United States. The scientific knowledge and the means of implementing it are out there in the world. Many countries have already built these weapons, and nuclear proliferation increases the likelihood that they may fall into ever more irresponsible hands.

There is plenty to fear when hundreds of millions of people feel so desperate and angry that they might be willing to use such weapons. The error in the reasoning behind the "war on terror" is that this nightmare scenario cannot be prevented by the United States imposing itself on one country after another in the Middle East and in every other area where terrorists might be able to steal or develop nuclear weapons. . . .

You Cannot Fight Terror with War

The whole notion of a war on terrorism is fundamentally misguided. Terrorism is a tactic used by people who do not have the powerful armies of the world at their disposal, and hence they will use homemade or stolen weapons against those who they believe to be oppressing them. If you have a population of 6.7 billion on the planet, the only way to absolutely control terrorism is to put surveillance devices into every home in the world so that everyone is so terrified of the police and so scared to express their anger that they have no possibility of resorting to terror. In that case—total fascism—the solution is far worse than the problem.

The obvious alternative is to address the grievances and problems that lead people to want to strike out against the West in general and the United States in particular. We've mentioned these in past editorials:

1. The Western impact on traditional societies has been destructive. While helping to develop a small middle class, the penetration of American corporations, the Western global media, and the capitalist marketplace have fostered an ethos of individualism, materialism, and selfishness. This is correctly perceived as having partially destroyed the religions and forms of cultural/communal solidarity within which people felt a sense of higher purpose and meaning to their lives. We recognize that many traditional societies have a strong downside, based as they are on authoritarian and patriarchal practices that are themselves oppressive. But the way to challenge those effectively is to support the development of spiritual and religious renewal that educates girls, empowers women, validates individual freedom within (not counterposed to) commitment to a community, and affirms the humanity of others in different spiritual and religious traditions. In short, we should actively support spiritual renewal, rather than attempt to replace traditional religions with the religion of the capitalist marketplace.

We cannot beat fundamentalism through consumer materialism and the ethos of "looking out for number one." This is especially true because of the changes that accompany such materialism and selfishness: the weakening of family ties; the prevalence of pornography and cheapening of sex into another commodity for sale and manipulation in the competitive marketplace; the elimination of any kind of economic safety net provided by people who genuinely care about you; and the obliteration of spiritual consciousness in favor of a one-dimensional version of technocratic rationality in which the accumulation of money and power is seen as the only real value in life. These changes are sure to evoke a powerful, angry, and at times violent response from those who have benefited from living in communities in which caring for each other has been part of their daily

Foreign ministers attend a counterterrorism United Nations Security Council meeting. Some believe that the UN should be the only international force to combat terrorism.

lives. If the alternative to fundamentalism is subjugation to Western values and to Western military and economic domination, people will take up arms and they will find a way to reach the United States with terrorist violence. These same concerns play out in a different but potentially just as violent way inside some parts of the United States itself, when right-wingers articulate this anger—ignoring how the social alienation and disintegration they rightly lament is rooted in the capitalist marketplace they champion—and then seek to channel that anger against liberals and enlightenment values, even at times advocating violence against President Obama.

2. Moreover, even those who are not motivated primarily by a desire to resist Western forms of modernization are moved to violence by the effects of capitalist economic penetration. One need only look at the huge belts of poverty in the ghettos and barrios of major cities around the world to see the degree of hunger and malnutrition, to recognize the growing prostitution of young girls and boys desperately seeking to feed their families, and to witness the hundreds of millions of economic migrants and refugees seeking some place to make a living. These victims

of our global economic arrangements are sitting ducks for ideologies that preach anger and violence against those Western powers that are seen as arrogantly ignoring this suffering. The fundamental disrespect and even humiliation that people in traditional societies experience when their own children begin to respond to the ethos of the marketplace, breaking away from traditional families so that they can sell themselves through prostitution or through pursuing self-interest and material gain at the expense of their connections to traditional spiritual communities, cannot be underestimated. Extremist forms of fundamentalist Islam or other forms of religious or political ideologies will spread and provide people with a way to express their anger at the West.

3. While claiming to bring democracy, we've simply imposed governments that agree to protect American corporate power. The Karzai government in Afghanistan tried to steal its recent election and proclaim itself a democracy—but fooled no one. The Iraqi democracy was imposed under occupation by U.S. troops and is unlikely to sustain itself once the United States really withdraws (not just its combat troops, but also the 80,000 "advisers" and countless independent contractors from the West). So while the West pretends that its mission is humanistic and aimed at spreading democracy and human rights, its hypocrisy becomes evident, thereby fueling people's willingness to engage in violence against those who are perceived as occupiers.

Champions of the war in Afghanistan willfully ignore all this. They imagine that all this anger can be contained by yet another military intervention. They ignore the history of the Afghanis' successful resistance to one foreign occupier after another, including the British and the Soviets. They refuse to acknowledge to themselves that the U.S. occupation of Iraq increased the violence of civil war, providing the weapons that Iraqis might have had no other way to obtain.

War is not the answer, and certainly not a war run by the United States.

Fight Terror with Police, Not War

The first step that is needed is to abandon the notion of a "war on terrorism." Drop it. Proclaim it already won. Or more honestly, acknowledge that there never can be a war against terrorism because terrorism is a tactic—the tactic of attacking civilians to spread fear. And that tactic has been used by the United States in Iraq, Afghanistan, Pakistan, and many other places in the world.

The second step is to replace the notion of war with the notion of police actions aimed at protecting people from organized bunches of criminals who seek to terrorize domestic populations or to impose their own religious, political, or economic rule on local communities that do not want that rule. The creation of an international police force of this sort, charged also with protecting development projects to improve the quality of life of people on the village and small-town level, should be given the highest priority. Moreover, representatives of countries that together represent the majority of the citizens of the world must be significantly involved in the formulation of this force.

> **FAST FACT**
>
> A 2010 CNN poll found that 60 percent of Americans think that terrorists will always find a way to launch major attacks no matter what the U.S. government does to prevent them.

We should try to get this created through the United Nations: not a toothless police force like those which have characterized the UN presence in Sudan, Rwanda, and the Congo, but a force that has a mandate to use all appropriate means to protect citizens against the harassment and oppression imposed by groups like the Taliban [a Sunni Islamist political movement]. But if there is no such willingness on the part of these countries to participate in creating and financing such a police force, the United States and other Western countries should not step into that space but should instead focus on defending their own borders, while continuing to beg the peoples of the world to step up and share the responsibility for creating an international police force whose sole aim is to protect local communities from the violence of those who seek to impose their rule by force.

Adopting a Strategy of Nonproliferation and Generosity

The third step is for the nuclear states to eliminate nuclear weapons. A careful global effort to protect every nuclear facility and to govern the creation and production of nuclear power should replace nuclear proliferation—but this will never happen if the nuclear states retain their own nuclear stashes. What, for instance, could possibly induce Arab states or Iran to eliminate the possibility of nuclear weapons when they know that Israel has close to 200 such weapons of its own, which it may rely on in case of war? Or what could induce India or Pakistan to reduce their nuclear arsenals as long as they fear each other's—or China's—nuclear weapons? As long as the current nuclear powers retain their weapons, proliferation is inevitable, and with it comes the danger of crazies obtaining those weapons and using them in terrorist attacks.

The fourth step is for the advanced industrial societies, led by the United States, to launch immediately a Domestic and Global Marshall Plan that would dedicate between 2 percent and 5 percent of their gross domestic product each year for the next twenty to once and for all end global poverty, homelessness, hunger, inadequate education, and inadequate health care, and to repair the global environment. We've outlined a way to do this that would avoid the corruption that has bedeviled various aid plans, as well as prevent the mistaken allocation of this aid to ruling elites, thus ensuring that the aid goes toward building the economic, educational, and health infrastructures that could succeed in permanently defeating global poverty. This step must be taken alongside of and with equal priority to the first three steps, and not as an afterthought or delayed till the other steps are shown to be effective, because they will not succeed unless they are accompanied by this step and its explicit articulation of an alternative worldview. . . .

A New Approach Is Needed

In short, we either pursue the same old ethically, environmentally, and economically destructive policies of war, or we embrace a new path of fundamental change. This new path should be based in part on repentance and atonement for how we have gone wrong. And it should replace the capitalist ethos of looking out for number one and the commitment to "progress" (understood as the endless accumulation of new material goods and electronic gadgets) with a new ethos of love, generosity, ecological sanity, and awe and wonder at the grandeur of the universe.

EVALUATING THE AUTHORS' ARGUMENTS:

Michael Lerner argues that war is the wrong format for addressing the problem of terrorism. How do you think each of the other authors in this chapter would respond to this idea? Write one paragraph for each author, then state what you think.

Chapter 3

How Should Suspected Terrorists Be Treated?

A U.S. soldier keeps watch at the terrorist detention center at Guantánamo Bay. Much controversy has arisen over treatment of terrorist suspects.

Harsh Interrogation Techniques Should Be Used on Suspected Terrorists

Deroy Murdock

"Water-boarding is something of which every American should be proud."

In the following viewpoint Deroy Murdock argues that harsh interrogation techniques should be used on suspected terrorists. He discusses the controversial technique of waterboarding in which a suspect is held underwater for several minutes to create the sensation of drowning. Murdock says there is no real threat from being waterboarded—though the process is definitely uncomfortable and scary, the person being interrogated is not in any true physical danger. Murdock thinks this is an appropriate way to treat people who would kill innocent American men, women, and children. In addition,

Murdock says, terrorists who have been waterboarded have yielded valuable information about other terrorists, in effect helping authorities prevent thousands of Americans from being killed in attacks. Murdock concludes it is better to make suspected terrorists uncomfortable for a while than for Americans to risk undergoing another massive terrorist attack.

Murdock is a columnist and a media fellow at the Hoover Institution, a think tank at Stanford University dedicated to research in domestic policy and international affairs.

AS YOU READ, CONSIDER THE FOLLOWING QUESTIONS:
1. According to the author, for how long did authorities waterboard terrorist Khalid Sheik Mohammed before he talked?
2. Who is Iyman Faris and how does Murdock factor him into his argument?
3. Who is Majid Khan and what does Murdock say he is suspected of?

It's not quite torture, but it sure has been painful watching Senate Democrats tie attorney general–designate Michael Mukasey into knots over waterboarding. Responding to their demands that he denounce this interrogation method that simulates drowning, Mukasey last Tuesday [October 30, 2007] declared that "these techniques seem over the line, or, on a personal basis, repugnant to me." Mukasey declined further comment because "I have not been briefed on techniques used in any classified interrogation program conducted by any government agency."

This left Judiciary Committee Democrats, including Illinois's Dick Durbin, unimpressed, putting Mukasey's confirmation bid in jeopardy.

"I can't support his nomination based on the letter he sent yesterday," Durbin said Wednesday. "It was a real disappointment."

Mukasey is at risk largely because, for years, the White House barely has replied to its critics' never-ending "torture" narrative. Cryptic statements, such as President [George W.] Bush's comment that "This government does not torture people," don't cut it.

Americans Should Be Proud of Waterboarding

While the White House must beware not to inform our enemies what to expect if captured, today's clueless anti-waterboarding rhetoric merits this tactic's vigorous defense. Waterboarding is something of which every American should be proud.

Waterboarding makes tight-lipped terrorists talk. At least three major al-Qaeda leaders reportedly have been waterboarded, most notably Khalid Sheik Mohammed.

KSM, as intelligence agencies call him, directed the September 11 attacks, which killed 2,978 people and injured at least 7,356. "I am the head of the al-Qaeda military committee," he told *Al Jazeera* in April 2002. "And yes, we did it." KSM wired money to his nephew, Ramzi Yousef, who masterminded the February 1993 World Trade Center blast that killed six and wounded 1,040. KSM and Yousef planned Operation Bojinka, a foiled 1995 scheme to explode 12 American jetliners above the Pacific. While some doubt his claim, KSM reportedly said, "I decapitated with my blessed right hand the head of the American Jew Daniel Pearl in the City of Karachi, Pakistan."

> **FAST FACT**
>
> A December 2009 Rasmussen Reports survey found that 58 percent of Americans think that waterboarding and other aggressive interrogation techniques should be used to gain information from captured terrorists.

Waterboarding Gets Results

U.S. and Pakistani authorities captured KSM on March 1, 2003 in Rawalpindi, Pakistan. KSM stayed mum for months, often answering questions with Koranic chants. Interrogators eventually waterboarded him—for just 90 seconds.

KSM "didn't resist," one CIA veteran said in the August 13 [2007] issue of *The New Yorker*. "He sang right away. He cracked real quick." Another CIA official told ABC News: "KSM lasted the longest under waterboarding, about a minute and a half, but once he broke, it never had to be used again."

KSM's revelations helped authorities identify and incarcerate at least six major terrorists:

- Ohio-based trucker Iyman Faris pleaded guilty May 1, 2003 to providing material support to terrorists. He secured 2,000 sleeping bags for al-Qaeda and delivered cash, cell phones, and airline tickets to its men. He also conspired to derail a train near Washington, D.C. and use acetylene torches to sever the Brooklyn Bridge's cables, plunging it into the East River.
- Jemaah Islamiya (JI) agent Rusman "Gun Gun" Gunawan was convicted of transferring money to bomb Jakarta's Marriott Hotel, killing 12 and injuring 150.
- Hambali, Gunawan's brother and ringleader of JI's October 2002 Bali nightclub blasts, killed 202 and wounded 209.
- Suspected al-Qaeda agent Majid Khan, officials say, provided money to JI terrorists and plotted to assassinate Pakistani president Pervez Musharraf, detonate U.S. gas stations, and poison American water reservoirs.
- Jose Padilla, who trained with al-Qaeda in Afghanistan, was convicted last August of providing material support to terrorists and conspiring to kidnap, maim, and murder people overseas. Padilla, suspected of but not charged with planning a radioactive "dirty bomb" attack, reportedly learned to incinerate residential highrises by igniting apartments filled with natural gas.
- Malaysian Yazid Sufaat, an American-educated biochemist and JI member, reportedly provided hijackers Khalid al-Midhar and Nawaf al-Hazmi housing in Kuala Lumpur during a January 2000 9-11 planning summit. He also is suspected of employing "20th hijacker" Zacarias Moussaoui. Page 151 of *The 9-11 Commission Report* states: "Sufaat would spend several months attempting to cultivate anthrax for al Qaeda in a laboratory he helped set up near the Kandahar airport."

Interrogating Terrorists Prevents Attacks

Imagine how many innocent people these six Islamo-fascists (and perhaps others) would have murdered, had interrogators left KSM unwaterboarded and his secrets unuttered.

"The most important source of intelligence we had after 9/11 came from the interrogation of high-value detainees," Robert Grenier, former chief of the CIA's Counterterrorism Center, told *The New*

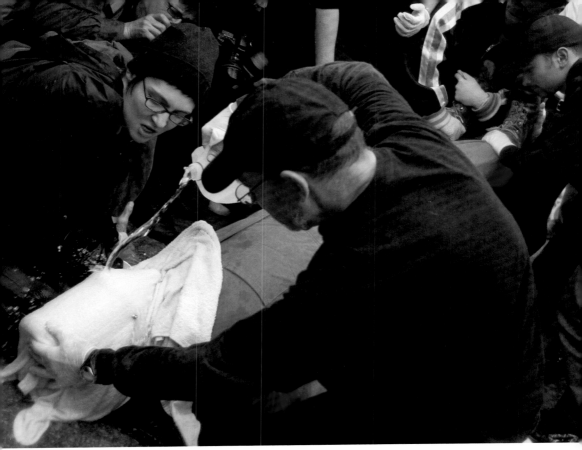

Protesters perform a simulation of the controversial waterboarding technique.

Yorker's Jane Mayer. He called KSM "the most valuable of the high-value detainees, because he had operational knowledge."

Meanwhile, President Bush is deeply deluded if he thinks opposing waterboarding will buy him any goodwill among the domestic and international Left, who hate him immeasurably. More quickly than the average Capitol Hill flip flop, Democrats who scream against waterboarding today will skin Bush alive if, God forbid, there is another major terror strike here on his watch.

"He didn't keep us safe," they will moan. "Why didn't he stop this?" they will bellow. Instantly forgotten will be Bush's very dangerous concessions to his domestic critics. His approval of the CIA's 2006 request to ban waterboarding will give Bush absolutely zero protection if today's soft-on-terror Democrats become tomorrow's post-attack hawks. They will pick him apart like a hummingbird.

Harsh Interrogation Methods are Needed During War

A 2009 poll found that even though 60 percent of Americans think waterboarding and other procedures qualify as torture, the majority approve of their use to get information out of suspected terrorists.

"Does waterboarding qualify as torture?"

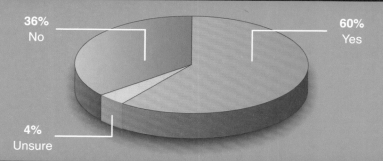

36%
No

60%
Yes

4%
Unsure

"Do you approve of the government decision to use such techniques?"

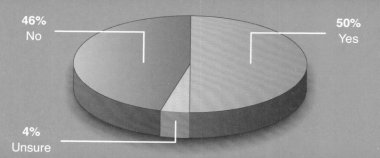

46%
No

50%
Yes

4%
Unsure

"Should officials who authorized such techniques be prosecuted?"

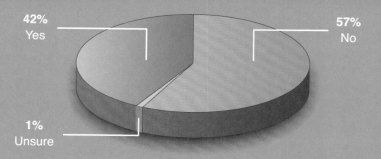

42%
Yes

57%
No

1%
Unsure

Taken from: CNN/Opinion Research poll, April 23–26, 2009.

This is all the more reason for President Bush to reinstate waterboarding, proudly and publicly, so America can get the information we need to prevent Muslim-fanatic mass murder and win the Global War on Terror.

Better to Stress Terrorists Than Americans

Appropriately enough, waterboarding is not used on American citizens suspected of tax evasion, sexual harassment, or bank robbery. Waterboarding is used on foreign Islamic-extremist terrorists, captured abroad, who would love nothing more than to blast innocent men, women, and children into small, bloody pieces. Some of them already have done so.

Waterboarding has worked quickly, causing at least one well-known subject to break down and identify at least six other high-profile, highly bloodthirsty associates before they could commit further mass murder beyond the 3,192 people they already killed and the 7,715 they already wounded.

Though clearly uncomfortable, waterboarding loosens lips without causing permanent physical injuries (and unlikely even temporary ones). If terrorists suffer long-term nightmares about waterboarding, better that than more Americans crying themselves to sleep after their loved ones have been shredded by bombs or baked in skyscrapers.

In short, there is nothing "repugnant" about waterboarding.

EVALUATING THE AUTHOR'S ARGUMENTS:

Murdock believes the United States must be aggressive if it is to prevent another terrorist attack, and this includes using harsh interrogation techniques to get information out of suspected terrorists. What do you think? Does harshly interrogating terrorists keep the United States safe or does it put it at even greater risk for being attacked? Explain your opinion using evidence from the texts you have read.

Viewpoint

2

Harsh Interrogation Techniques Should Not Be Used on Suspected Terrorists

Christopher Hitchens

Christopher Hitchens is a journalist whose articles have appeared in *Vanity Fair* and other publications. In the following viewpoint he describes how he volunteered to be waterboarded to gain better insight into whether the interrogation technique qualifies as torture. Hitchens says waterboarding was one of the most terrifying experiences of his life—had he been a suspected terrorist undergoing the procedure for real, he would have told his captors anything they wanted to know. But this, says Hitchens, is part of the problem—torture is a notoriously bad way to extract information from someone. They end up saying anything, even lies, just to make the torture

"If water-boarding does not constitute torture, then there is no such thing as torture."

stop. Furthermore, if the United States becomes known as a torturer, Hitchens worries that captured U.S. soldiers will be subject to torture. For these and other reasons, Hitchens says waterboarding should be considered a form of torture and should not be allowed to be used on suspected terrorists.

AS YOU READ, CONSIDER THE FOLLOWING QUESTIONS:
1. In a few sentences, describe the process of waterboarding as Hitchens says he experienced it.
2. What does Hitchens say one person falsely confessed to being after experiencing waterboarding?
3. What does Hitchens mean when he says waterboarding "opens a door that cannot be closed"?

On a gorgeous day last May [2007] I found myself deep in the hill country of western North Carolina, preparing to be surprised by a team of extremely hardened veterans who had confronted their country's enemies in highly arduous terrain all over the world. They knew about everything from unarmed combat to enhanced interrogation and, in exchange for anonymity, were going to show me as nearly as possible what real waterboarding might be like.

Waterboarding Can Cause Death

It goes without saying that I knew I could stop the process at any time, and that when it was all over I would be released into happy daylight rather than returned to a darkened cell. But it's been well said that cowards die many times before their deaths, and it was difficult for me to completely forget the clause in the contract of indemnification that I had signed. This document (written by one who knew) stated revealingly:

> "Water boarding" is a potentially dangerous activity in which the participant can receive serious and permanent (physical, emotional and psychological) injuries and even death, including injuries and death due to the respiratory and neurological systems of the body.

As the agreement went on to say, there would be safeguards provided "during the 'water boarding' process, however, these measures may fail and even if they work properly they may not prevent Hitchens from experiencing serious injury or death." . . .

A Journalist Undergoes Waterboarding

I was very gently yet firmly grabbed from behind, pulled to my feet, pinioned by my wrists (which were then cuffed to a belt), and cut

Essayist Christopher Hitchens volunteered himself to be waterboarded and is adamant that it is torture.

off from the sunlight by having a black hood pulled over my face. I was then turned around a few times, I presume to assist in disorienting me, and led over some crunchy gravel into a darkened room. Well, mainly darkened: there were some oddly spaced bright lights that came as pinpoints through my hood. And some weird music assaulted my ears. (I'm no judge of these things, but I wouldn't have expected former Special Forces types to be so fond of New Age techno-disco.) The outside world seemed very suddenly very distant indeed.

Arms already lost to me, I wasn't able to flail as I was pushed onto a sloping board and positioned with my head lower than my heart. (That's the main point: the angle can be slight or steep.) Then my legs were lashed together so that the board and I were one single and trussed unit. Not to bore you with my phobias, but if I don't have at least two pillows I wake up with acid reflux and mild sleep apnea, so even a merely supine position makes me uneasy. And, to tell you something I had been keeping from myself as well as from my new experimental friends, I do have a fear of drowning that comes from a bad childhood moment on the Isle of Wight, when I got out of my depth. As a boy reading the climactic torture scene of [the dystopian novel] *1984*, where what is in Room 101 is the worst thing in the world, I realize that somewhere in my version of that hideous chamber comes the moment when the wave washes over me. Not that that makes me special: I don't know anyone who *likes* the idea of drowning. As mammals we may have originated in the ocean, but water has many ways of reminding us that when we are in it we are out of our element. In brief, when it comes to breathing, give me good old air every time.

Flooded with Panic and Terror

You may have read by now the official lie about this treatment, which is that it "simulates" the feeling of drowning. This is not the

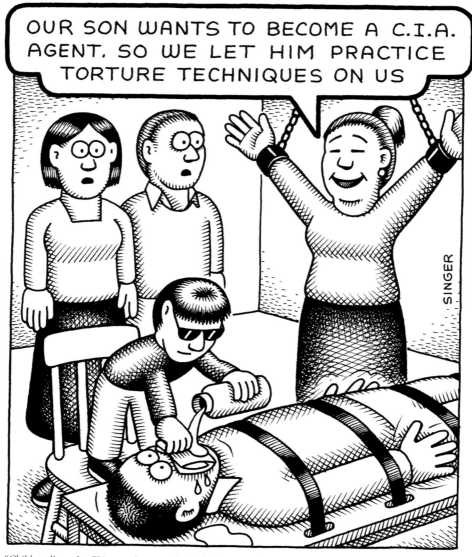

OUR SON WANTS TO BECOME A C.I.A. AGENT. SO WE LET HIM PRACTICE TORTURE TECHNIQUES ON US

SINGER

"Child studies to be CIA agent," cartoon by Andy Singer, PoliticalCartoons.com, February 12, 2008.

case. You feel that you are drowning because you *are* drowning—or, rather, being drowned, albeit slowly and under controlled conditions and at the mercy (or otherwise) of those who are applying the pressure. The "board" is the instrument, *not* the method. You are not being boarded. You are being watered. This was very rapidly brought home to me when, on top of the hood, which still admitted a few flashes of random and worrying strobe light to my vision, three layers of enveloping towel were added. In this pregnant darkness, head downward, I waited for a while until I abruptly felt a slow cascade of water going up my nose. Determined to resist if only for the honor of my navy ancestors who had so often been in peril on the sea, I held my breath for a while and then had to exhale and—as you might expect—inhale in turn. The inhalation brought the damp cloths tight against my nostrils, as if a huge, wet paw had been suddenly and annihilatingly clamped over my face. Unable to determine whether I was breathing in or out, and flooded more with sheer panic than with mere water, I triggered the pre-arranged signal and felt the unbelievable relief of being pulled upright and having the soaking and stifling layers pulled off me. I find I don't want to tell you how little time I lasted. . . .

Waterboarding Is Definitely Torture

An interval was ordered, and then I felt the mask come down again. Steeling myself to remember what it had been like last time, and to learn from the previous panic attack, I fought down the first, and some of the second, wave of nausea and terror but soon found that I was an abject prisoner of my gag reflex. The interrogators would hardly have had time to ask me any questions, and I knew that I would quite readily have agreed to supply any answer. I still feel ashamed when I think about it. Also, in case it's of interest, I have since woken up trying to push the bedcovers off my face, and if I do anything that makes me short of breath I find myself clawing at the air with a horrible sensation of smothering and claustrophobia. No doubt this will pass. As if detecting my misery and shame, one of my interrogators comfortingly said, "Any time is a long time when you're breathing water." I could have hugged him for saying so, and just then I was hit with a ghastly sense of the sadomasochistic [deriving pleasure from inflicting physical or mental pain on others or oneself] dimension that underlies the relationship between the torturer and the tortured. I apply the Abraham Lincoln test for moral casuistry: "If slavery is not wrong, nothing is wrong." Well, then, if waterboarding does not constitute torture, then there is no such thing as torture. . . .

Torture Yields Bad Intelligence

The argument [against using torture] goes like this:

1. Waterboarding is a deliberate torture technique and has been prosecuted as such by our judicial arm when perpetrated by others.
2. If we allow it and justify it, we cannot complain if it is employed in the future by other regimes on captive U.S. citizens. It is a method of putting American prisoners in harm's way.
3. It may be a means of extracting information, but it is also a means of extracting junk information. ([One expert] told me that he had heard of someone's being compelled to confess that he was a hermaphrodite [having both male and female reproductive organs]. I later had an awful twinge while wondering if I myself could have been "dunked" this far.) To put it briefly, even the C.I.A. sources for the *Washington Post* story on waterboarding conceded that the information they got out of Khalid Sheikh Mohammed was "not all of it reliable." Just put a pencil line under that last phrase, or commit it to memory.
4. It opens a door that cannot be closed. Once you have posed the notorious "ticking bomb" question, and once you assume that you are in the right, what will you *not* do? Waterboarding not getting results fast enough? The terrorist's clock still ticking? Well, then, bring on the thumbscrews and the pincers and the electrodes and the rack.

EVALUATING THE AUTHORS' ARGUMENTS:

In this viewpoint Christopher Hitchens categorizes waterboarding as torture. In the previous viewpoint, Deroy Murdock classifies it as an uncomfortable yet effective technique for preventing terrorism. After reading both viewpoints, how would you describe waterboarding? Would you classify it as torture or as merely uncomfortable? Do you think it should be used on suspected terrorists? Quote from both texts in your answer.

Viewpoint

3

Terrorists Should Be Tried in Civilian Courts

"We hold trials in public not only because we want a check on the government's behavior but because a key part of the exercise is a public accounting and condemnation of wrongs."

Josh Marshall

In the following viewpoint Josh Marshall argues that terrorists should be openly tried in public civilian courts rather than private military ones. He argues that civilian courts are unlikely to unjustly protect terrorists or acquit any truly guilty terrorist of his crimes. It is possible that during the course of such a trial, negative things about the United States might come to light—such as the possibility that some terrorist suspects have been tortured in U.S. custody—but Marshall says such events are already public knowledge and are not going to be made worse if said aloud in court. Furthermore, Marshall thinks it is unlikely that terrorists will escape and cause further harm to residents of New York, where such trials would take place. He concludes the concerns of those against civilian terrorist trials are unfounded and argues the best thing for

Josh Marshall, "Why Is It a Problem?" *TalkingPointsMemo.com,* November 16, 2009. Copyright © 2009 TPM Media LLC. Reproduced by permission of the author.

the government, the public, and the 9/11 terrorists is to try suspected criminals in full view of the public.

Marshall is editor and publisher of TalkingPointsMemo.com, an online investigative news magazine.

AS YOU READ, CONSIDER THE FOLLOWING QUESTIONS:
1. In the context of this viewpoint, what does the author mean by the phrase "untainted evidence"?
2. With regard to trying terrorists in civilian courts, what risk does Marshall say does not appear to exist?
3. What does Marshall say makes him doubt that any harm would come to New Yorkers if terrorists were tried in that city?

A lot of people—mainly but by no means exclusively Republicans—were on the Sunday shows yesterday [November 15, 2009] denouncing the administration's decision to jail and try KSM[1] and four accused 9/11 plotters in New York City. And most of the criticism comes under three distinct but related arguments: 1) civilian trials give the defendants too many rights and protections and thus create too big a risk they'll get acquitted and set free, 2) holding the prisoners and trial in New York City puts the city's civilian population at unnecessary risk of new terror attacks, and 3) holding public, civilian trials will give the defendants an opportunity to mock the victims, have a platform to issue propaganda or gain public sympathy.

The first two arguments strike me as understandable but basically wrong on the facts. The third I find difficult in some ways even to understand and seems grounded in bad political values or even ideological cowardice.

Terror Suspects Are Unlikely to Be Acquitted

Let's start with the idea that civilian trials have too many safeguards and create too big a risk these guys will go free. This does not hold up to any scrutiny for two reasons. First, remember all those high-

1. Khalid Sheikh Mohammed, mastermind of the 9/11 attacks.

profile terror prosecutions where the defendants went free? Right, me neither. It just does not happen. The fact is that federal judges are extremely deferential to the government in terror prosecutions. And national security law already gives the government the ability to do lots of things the government would never be allowed to do in a conventional civilian trial. (People who really think this is an issue seem to base their understanding of federal criminal procedure on watching too many Dirty Harry movies, which, as it happens, I'm actually a big fan of. But remember, they're movies.) KSM is not going to be able to depose or cross-examine CIA Director Leon Panetta or President [George W.] Bush or Vice President [Dick] Cheney or anyone else.

The possibility that a judge would suppress evidence obtained through torture is a real one. But [Attorney General] Eric Holder made clear he and his prosecutors believe they have more than enough untainted evidence to obtain convictions. So that should not be an issue.

U.S. attorney general Eric Holder defends his decision to prosecute alleged terrorists in civilian courts in testimony before the Senate Judiciary Committee.

"It's Simply Not Going to Happen"

Finally, even in the extremely unlikely case that any of the five were acquitted of these charges, the government has a hundred other things it can charge them with. Indeed, the government could as easily turn them over to military commissions or indefinite detention post-acquittal as it can do those things with them now. That may not make civil libertarians happy. But it is the nail in the coffin of any suggestions that these guys are going to be walking out of the federal courthouse in lower Manhattan saying they're headed to Disneyland. It's simply not going to happen.

(The best argument against what I've argued here is probably the case of El Sayyid Nosair, the murderer of Jewish extremist leader Meir Kahane, who received a partial acquittal when he was tried in 1991. Here I would say that the case came prior to modern counter-terrorism law in the United States, which I'd date to the first World Trade Center bombing in 1993. And the Nosair example actually proves my larger point since a subsequent terrorism conspiracy trial got Nosair a life without parole plus fifteen year sentence, which he is now serving at the SuperMax facility in Florence, Colorado.)

FAST FACT

According to the New York University Center for Law and Security, since 2001 the criminal courts have convicted more than 150 suspects on terrorism charges.

We can imagine a different set of facts, where all the most damning evidence was obtained through torture, and acquittal seemed at all a reasonable possibility. In that case there might be a real question as to whether it was worth taking the risk when military commissions which have been used in the past are available. But this 'risk' simply doesn't appear to exist so you do not even need to get to the constitutional or deeper rule-of-law questions.

There Is No Danger to New Yorkers

Next we have the question of danger to the people of New York City. As I said in my first post on this question, just on the facts I don't think al Qaeda terrorists are holding off on attacking New York now because they lack incentive or feel we haven't pushed things far

Results of Terrorism-Associated Prosecutions

As of September 2009, the Department of Justice has indicted 828 people suspected of terrorism and prosecuted 593 of them. About 88 percent of those tried were convicted on charges of terrorism, national security violations, or other crimes.

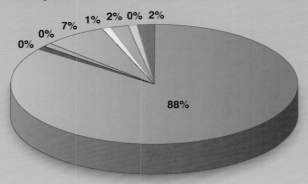

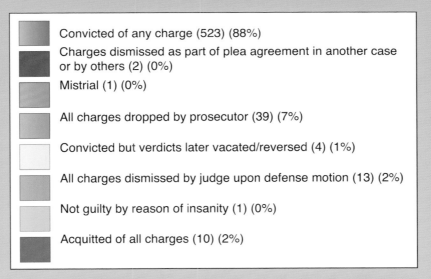

(593 resolved prosecutions)

	Convicted of any charge (523) (88%)
	Charges dismissed as part of plea agreement in another case or by others (2) (0%)
	Mistrial (1) (0%)
	All charges dropped by prosecutor (39) (7%)
	Convicted but verdicts later vacated/reversed (4) (1%)
	All charges dismissed by judge upon defense motion (13) (2%)
	Not guilty by reason of insanity (1) (0%)
	Acquitted of all charges (10) (2%)

Taken from: *Terrorism Trial Report Card, September 11, 2001–September 11, 2009*, Center on Law and Security, January 2010, p.2.

enough yet to merit another hit. The symbolic value of hitting New York might increase a bit. But it's already so high for these people that the increase seems notional at best. And more to the point, I choose to trust the people already charged with keeping the city safe.

On a more general level, however, since when is it something we advertise or say proudly that we're going to change our behavior because we fear terrorists will attack us if we don't? To be unPC [unpolitically correct] about it, isn't there some residual national machismo that keeps us from cowering even before trivially increased dangers? As much as I think the added dangers are basically nil, I'm surprised that people can stand up and say we should change what we do in response to some minuscule added danger and not be embarrassed.

Terrorist Testimony Will Not Hurt America

And finally we come to the fear of what KSM and the others will say. I don't see what factual dispute there is here. And at some level I don't even understand the argument. Logically I understand it; I understand what they're saying. But it's so contrary to my values and assumptions that at some level I don't get it. I cannot imagine anything KSM or his confederates would say that would diminish America or damage us in any way. Are we really so worried that what we represent is so questionable or our identity so brittle? (Some will say, yes: torture. The fact that some of these men were tortured is a huge stain on the country. But it happened and it's known about. To the extent that it is a stain it is the kind of stain that is diminished not made worse by an open public accounting.) Does anyone think that Nuremberg trials[2] or the trial of [Nazi] Adolph Eichmann in Jerusalem in 1961 or the war crimes trials of [former Yugoslav president] Slobodan Milosevic and others at the Hague advanced these mens' causes? Or that, in retrospect, it would have been wiser to hold these trials in secret?

At the end of the day, what are we afraid these men are going to say?

Do Not Forget the Purpose of a Trial

What we seem to be forgetting here is that trials are not simply for judging guilt and meting out punishment. We hold trials in public not only because we want a check on the government's behavior but because a key part of the exercise is a public accounting and condem-

2. The trials in which prominent Nazis were prosecuted for war crimes after World War II.

nation of wrongs. Especially in great trials for the worst crimes they are public displays pitting one set of values against another. And I'm troubled by anyone who thinks that this is a confrontation in which we would come out the worse.

EVALUATING THE AUTHORS' ARGUMENTS:

Marshall believes that trying terrorists openly in civilian courts is an excellent way to show the government has nothing to hide about the way it has treated the suspects in its custody. Rowan Scarborough, author of the following viewpoint, disagrees, saying that trying terrorists in civilian courts invites inappropriate criticism of the way the government has handled itself in the war on terror. After reading both viewpoints, with which author do you agree, and why?

Terrorists Should Not Be Tried In Civilian Courts

Rowan Scarborough

"[Khalid Sheikh Mohammed] is an individual who is accused of being a war criminal, as opposed to a domestic criminal."

Rowan Scarborough discusses reasons why captured al Qaeda terrorists should not be tried in civilian courts. These reasons include providing an opportunity for the defendants to proclaim their views to the world, trying a person guilty of a war crime in a civilian court, the potential for the release of classified information, the risk of an acquittal based on legal technicalities appropriate for civilian criminal cases, the attention of the media, and the costs associated with a civilian trial. As an alternative, Scarborough supports the trial of al Qaeda terrorists before a military commission.

Rowan Scarborough is a national security writer who has written books on Donald Rumsfeld and the CIA, including the *New York Times* bestseller *Rumsfeld's War*.

AS YOU READ, CONSIDER THE FOLLOWING QUESTIONS:
  1. Who is Tom Hemingway, and what is his view on how al Qaeda terrorists should be tried, according to the author?
  2. What are two civilian court legal arguments that might enable an al Qaeda terrorist such as Khalid Sheikh Mohammed to go free, according to the viewpoint?
  3. Who is Tom McInerney, and what is his view on how al Qaeda terrorists should be tried, according to the author?

Khalid Sheikh Mohammed is coming to the Big Apple for trial, a move that opens up intelligence secrets to arch-enemy al Qaeda and tells American troops the war on terror is shifting back to a law enforcement exercise.

President Obama's decision to bring the 9-11 attack mastermind to a federal court house in New York, within blocks of the sacred ground that once braced the World Trade Center, also unleashes defense lawyers to put the United States on trial in the world's attention-getting media capital.

Instead of a more secretive military commission, as planned by President Bush for al Qaeda war criminals, the bearded, thobe-wearing Mohammed will sit in open court as civilian defense attorneys pound the government with motions to release sensitive material, suppress evidence and dismiss murder charges.

The people who worked to put the commission system in place under Defense Secretary Donald Rumsfeld told *Human Events* the president made a strategic mistake.

"I was disappointed in that decision simply because I think the 9-11 conspirators were clearly guilty of violations of the law of war," said retired Air Force Brig. Gen. Tom Hemingway, the military lawyer who advised the convening authority officer who oversaw the commission system.

"I think it's appropriate to try violations of the law of war in military commissions regardless of who the victims may have been," Hemingway told *Human Events*. "Having said that, where to try them is a policy decision. I don't think there is anything illegal in the president's decision to do that."

The majority of Americans favor using military tribunals to try suspected terrorists. They believe it will result in a more secure trial.

Question: "Which do you think is more important: to try 9/11 terror suspects in an open trial in civilian court so the world can see how the American system works, or to try 9/11 terror suspects in military courts to better assure security of trials?"

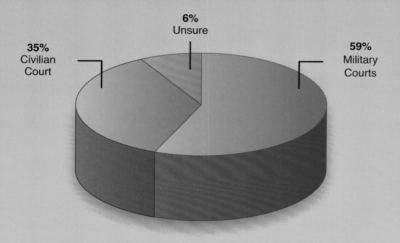

6%
Unsure

35%
Civilian
Court

59%
Military
Courts

Taken from: Quinnipiac University poll, February 2–8, 2010.

Of Mohammed, Hemingway said, "He is an individual who is accused of being a war criminal, as opposed to a domestic criminal. I think what we're doing here is treating him like a domestic criminal as opposed to a war criminal."

The shift in venue could not be more stark. New York City is a media magnet, while the isolated Guantanamo base would likely attract relatively fewer TV reporters. There is only one media travel route to Guantanamo, and the Pentagon owns the airline.

In a military commission, the confessed mass-murderer would be tried by U.S. officers as judge and jury. They would be expected to put strict limits on the public release of classified information.

The commission would have more leeway in allowing prosecution evidence, the same evidence a civilian federal judge might suppress. Mohammed was water-boarded (simulated drowning) to get him to talk. It is presumed CIA interrogators did not read him his Miranda rights, as is required by law enforcement investigators for civilian trial.

"There's a litigation risk of course," Hemingway said. "I'm assuming they have contemplated those risks and think they are willing to take."

Mohammed's defense team will now have a range of pre-trial legal issues to argue. Right off the bat, they may ask for dismissal based on a lack of speedy trial. The al Qaeda leader was captured six years ago.

"I expect there to be a range of motions from innovative defense counsel to get the charges dismissed and vigorously represent the client," retired Maj. Gen. Michael Nardotti, the Army's top lawyer in the 1990s, told *Human Events.* "I think speedy trial is an issue. In military commissions, the normal rules of search and seizure and advising a combatant of his rights would be specifically excluded. They are not in a federal court."

The prosecution's ace may turn out to be Mohammed himself. He proudly confessed to the horrible crime in open court at Guantanamo.

> **FAST FACT**
>
> A 2010 poll by Quinnipiac University found that the majority of Americans—59 percent—think terrorists should be tried in military rather than civilian courts.

"I think the statement would certainly be admissible," Hemingway said.

Larry Di Rita, a close adviser to secretary Rumsfeld when the commissions system was set up, told *Human Events,* "The use of commissions to render just decisions in wartime has a rich history in America's legal traditions. The use of the Article 3 courts does not. To me, that speaks volumes about the risks to this decision."

Article 3 refers to the section in the Constitution that established the Supreme Court and authorized Congress to set up the federal court system.

Obama is also taking heat from members of his own party.

Sen. Jim Webb, Virginia Democrat, said a civilian court trial will be costly and chaotic.

"It will be disruptive, costly, and potentially counterproductive to try them as criminals in our civilian courts," he said. "The precedent set by this decision deserves careful scrutiny as we consider proper venues for trying those now held at Guantanamo who were apprehended outside of this country for acts that occurred outside of the country. And we must be especially careful with any decisions to bring onto American soil any of those prisoners who remain a threat to our country but whose cases have been adjudged as inappropriate for trial at all. They do not belong in our country, they do not belong in our courts, and they do not belong in our prisons."

"I have consistently argued that military commissions, with the additional procedural rules added by Congress and enacted by President Obama, are the most appropriate venue for trying individuals adjudged to be enemy combatants."

Sen. John McCain, Arizona Republican and long a hawk on the war on terror, also said the president was making a mistake.

"Today's decision sends a mixed message about America's resolve in the fight against terrorism," he said. "We are at war, and we must bring terrorists to justice in a manner consistent with the horrific acts of war they have committed."

A criminal defense attorney said things could go terribly wrong in Manhattan.

"The danger is the potential that sources and methods of intelligence collection might be compromised in court," said Charles Gittins, a prominent civilian defense lawyer who has represented clients in a number of high-profile courts martial.

Gittins told *Human Events* there is a law, the Classified Information Procedure Act, prosecutors can cite to keep highly classified information away from the public—and our enemies. But the process increases the possibility such intelligence crown jewels will be leaked to the media.

"I would expect that there would be significant motions regarding the water boarding of KSM in order to obtain a confession," Gittins said. "I am not sure how you can conduct such a motion in secret

Terrorist suspect Khalid Sheikh Mohammed is arraigned before a U.S. military commission tribunal in January 2009. Many argue that terrorists should only be tried by the military.

outside the public view and even if you could, how that information would not eventually become public through leaks."

Gittins, a former Marine Corps aviator, said holding Mohammed in New York will enhance the city as a terror target. "Terrorists would use his place of detention as a target to 'make a statement' and strike at the U.S. and its justice system."

Then there is the military effect of moving Mohammed from the terrorists-designed prison at Guantanamo, to a jail cell where he will be among common criminals.

"I find it incomprehensible that we would turn the Global War on Terror [Bush's official designation] back into a law enforcement effort when we had almost 50 U.S. troops killed last month in Afghanistan," said retired Air Force Lt. Gen. Tom McInerney, a fighter pilot in Vietnam. "This sends a signal to radical Islamists that the Obama administration does not have the stomach for defeating them. It will embolden them and more American lives will be lost by this mockery of justice to those killed on 9/11. It will embolden Taliban and al Qaeda to use more aggressive suicide attacks against U.S. troops in order to discourage American people in the war against radical Islam. We are at war, Mr. President."

If a judge throws out the charges on a technicality, or a jury acquits Mohammed, the master terrorist, in theory, could catch a cab to John F. Kennedy airport and fly to whatever country would take him. Or maybe not.

Attorney General Eric Holder was vague at a Friday press conference when asked what happens if Mohammed beats the rap. The Bush administration had no intention of ever freeing Mohammed even if a military commission acquitted him.

"The prior administration's position was that we can hold detainees for as long as is necessary in a time of conflict, regardless of the outcome of the proceeding," Nardotti said. "So it will be interesting to see what the position is of the current administration. If it's dismissed at an earlier stage, is there going to be the option of then trying to take him back before the military commissions because jeopardy does not automatically attach?"

EVALUATING THE AUTHORS' ARGUMENTS:

In this viewpoint, Rowan Scarborough argues against trying terrorists in civilian court and in favor of trying them before a military commission. The author of the previous viewpoint, Josh Marshall, argues in favor of trying terrorists in a civilian court trial. Which author makes the better case? Support your view with evidence from each viewpoint.

Convicted Terrorists Should Get the Death Penalty

Stewart Weiss

"These monsters who specifically target civilians have no right to live. They have forfeited the most basic human privilege by virtue of their crimes."

In the following viewpoint Stewart Weiss argues that terrorists should be given the death penalty. Weiss, a rabbi who lives in Israel, describes how Palestinian terrorists have targeted Israelis during religious ceremonies, while at school, and in other noncombative environments. Their willingness to kill even children makes terrorists, in Weiss's opinion, monsters who have no regard for human life and thus do not deserve to live. He argues that executing a terrorist is the only way to guarantee that a terrorist will not be released from or escape from jail to kill again. In Weiss's opinion, executing terrorists also deters other terrorists from striking—he thinks it sends the message that terrorism is among society's most serious crimes and will not be taken lightly. For all these reasons, Weiss thinks convicted terrorists in both Israel and the United States should be given the death penalty.

Weiss is a rabbi, a columnist for the *Jerusalem Post*, and the director of the Ohel Ari Jewish Outreach Center in Ra'anana, Israel. His son, a soldier in the Israeli army, was killed in the line of duty in 2002.

AS YOU READ, CONSIDER THE FOLLOWING QUESTIONS:
1. What was the one case in which Israel enacted the death penalty, according to Weiss?
2. What does Weiss say is an "obscene insult" to people who have lost loved ones to terrorism?
3. What does Weiss say happened in Texas after the death penalty was reinstated there?

Desperate times call for drastic measures. The savage attacks which periodically target our civilian population bring home a terrible reality many of us already knew: The Palestinian terror machine has no red lines. Every gathering of Jews—anytime, anywhere—is a legitimate target for these sadistic haters; on a plane, at a Pessah [Passover] Seder, in a school library, a kindergarten or a hospital. There is no "Geneva Convention" to restrain them, no moral boundaries in which to confine their crimes.

Like Amalek[1] of old—the archetypal Jew-hater par excellence—these contemporary Hamans[2] prey upon the innocent as their primary targets.

Terrorists Cause Death and So Deserve Death

They enter hospitals with explosive-belts under their clothes; they lay in wait to shoot at passing cars; they blow up school buses as they load or unload their young passengers. And when they have perpetrated their "courageous" deeds, an ecstatic Palestine dances in the streets and hands out candies, displaying overwhelming, enthusiastic support for the outrage. Even the "moderate" Palestinians like Mahmoud Abbas mutter only the most tepid and half-hearted of condemnations, never declaring that the crime was wrong; saying only that "it hurts Palestinian interests."

1. Biblical figure who hated the Jews.
2. Haman was a biblical figure who sought the eradication of the Jews.

In such an environment, we must take drastic action. One of the things we can and should do is activate the death penalty—used just once in our history, when the architect of the Holocaust, Adolf Eichmann, was executed by hanging on June 1, 1962—against any terrorist who survives an attack, or against those who directly assist him in carrying out his crime.

The Death Penalty Is Unpopular but Not Always Wrong

Endorsing capital punishment is not very popular these days. The European Union bars member states from using the death penalty, and human rights activists scream bloody murder at the prospect of innocent people being wrongfully executed. Some religious leaders decry the unfairness of anyone taking a life other than the God who gave it (though they are strangely silent about euthanasia).

Jewish sources, too, tend to lean against capital punishment. The [Jewish book] Talmud calls a Jewish court that executes one person in 70 years a "bloody court." And Maimonides writes: "It is better to acquit a thousand guilty persons than to put a single innocent one to death." Yet the Talmud, not to mention the Torah, cites numerous occasions when criminals were indeed executed, ruling specifically that capital punishment can be instituted "when the times demand it."

FAST FACT

A 2009 *USA Today*/Gallup poll found that 77 percent of Americans think convicted terrorists should get the death penalty.

And in the United States—which suspended executions in 1973 but resumed them in 1977—a recent Gallup poll found that 60 percent of the population not only supports the death penalty, but believes the sentence is not being carried out often enough.

Terrorists Have No Right to Live

There are three compelling reasons why terrorists should be executed and, as in the Eichmann case, their remains cremated and unceremoniously dumped at sea in an unknown location. First and foremost is justice. Simply put, these monsters who specifically target civilians

Many Israelis want to institute the death penalty for convicted terrorists. Israel has executed only one person in its history—Nazi war criminal Adolf Eichmann (pictured, standing) in 1961.

have no right to live. They have forfeited the most basic human privilege by virtue of their crimes; any punishment save death is too good for them and is an obscene insult to the grieving victims of terror.

Secondly, killing a terrorist insures that he or she will not be committing any more murders. We have seen all too often how murderers are set free in this country after a relatively short time, only to kill many more innocents. As long as we have morally-misguided men in our government who, incredibly, go around calling for mass-murderers such as [Palestinian political leader] Marwan Barghouti to be freed in the name of "peace," we can never be sure that these criminals will stay behind bars. Unless we execute them.

Executing Terrorists Sends the Right Message

Finally, there is certainly an element of deterrence created by capital punishment. In America, a clear correlation has been shown between the number of executions and the concurrent decrease in homicides. The most striking example of this is in Texas, which executes more murderers than any other state. According to the Justice for All organization, the Texas murder rate fell by 60 percent after the state began to aggressively enforce capital punishment. And while Middle East terrorists often proclaim their willingness—even zeal—to be martyred, their accomplices in terror, and even they themselves may certainly be influenced by the knowledge that their lives will be forfeited for their crimes.

EVALUATING THE AUTHORS' ARGUMENTS:

Weiss claims that executing terrorists will deter other people from committing acts of terrorism because they will want to avoid being killed by the government. How would Michael C. Dorf, author of the following viewpoint, respond to this claim? Quote from both texts in your answer.

Convicted Terrorists Should Not Get the Death Penalty

Michael C. Dorf

"People who hope to succeed by dying are highly unlikely to worry about the possibility of being killed if they are captured."

In the following viewpoint Michael C. Dorf argues it does not make sense to give convicted terrorists the death penalty. Although death penalty supporters argue that capital punishment deters crime, Dorf argues it is unlikely that executing terrorists would deter any would-be terrorists. For one, terrorists usually plan on dying as part of their attack; Dorf says they would not care whether they would be killed if caught. Secondly, terrorists might even welcome death, as they typically seek to martyr themselves on behalf of their cause. Dorf says that even though the death penalty offers justice to some Americans, it is more likely to endanger other Americans by fanning flames of anti-Americanism and inspiring more terrorists to participate in acts of violence against the United States.

Dorf is a professor of law at Columbia University and the author of No Litmus Test: Law and Politics in the Twenty-First Century.

AS YOU READ, CONSIDER THE FOLLOWING QUESTIONS:
1. Who is Mohamed al-Qahtani and how does he factor into the author's argument?
2. In the context of the argument, what does Dorf mean by the term "vigilantism"?
3. Who is Donald Rumsfeld, and how does he factor into the author's argument?

Earlier this week [in February 2008] the [George W.] Bush Administration announced plans to seek the death penalty for Khalid Shaikh Mohammed and five other persons who allegedly played a role in the 9/11 attacks. The Administration plans to try the six defendants before military commissions, as authorized by the Military Commissions Act (MCA) of 2006. But the plan raises a host of difficult legal questions. . . .

The Death Penalty Will Not Deter Martyrs
Death penalty supporters sometimes point to deterrence as a basis for government imposition of the ultimate penalty. Whether the death penalty in fact deters crime is the subject of serious debate. Some recent studies claim to find a deterrent effect, while other scholars have pointed to flaws in the methodology of these studies that, the critics say, make the researchers' conclusions unreliable.

So, does the death penalty have a greater deterrent effect than the prospect of life imprisonment? Whatever the right answer to that question may be, the question of deterrence has a very different complexion when applied to terrorists whose very aim is to die while carrying out an attack on civilians. People who hope to succeed by dying are highly unlikely to worry about the possibility of being killed if they are captured.

Al Qaeda Terrorists Welcome Death
This logic applies most directly to Mohamed al-Qahtani, the alleged "twentieth hijacker," as he would have died in the 9/11 attacks if

he had successfully entered the United States in August 2001. One might think, however, that Khalid Shaikh Mohammed—the alleged mastermind of the attacks—and the five other defendants—who are alleged to have played supporting roles—were not planning to die, and thus that executing them after a guilty verdict would indeed be, for them, a punishment rather than vindication.

Yet for two reasons, this line of reasoning is faulty. First, whatever else one can say about al Qaeda [an Islamist terrorist group] operatives and their leadership, it is difficult to accuse them of insincerity. People who voluntarily forego comfortable lives to live in caves, fight in wars, and murder civilians in large numbers, all for the supposed glory of God, are deadly serious about their willingness, even eagerness, to become martyrs.

Second, even if a handful of al Qaeda members harbor doubts about the 72 virgins awaiting them in heaven, that fact would only be relevant to specific deterrence of those particular persons, but the core consequentialist argument for the death penalty is that it enhances general deterrence. In this view, terrorists at large will see the execution of Mohammed, al-Qahtani and the others, and abandon their nefarious plans for fear of a similar fate. Given the motivations and methods of terrorists, however, this scenario is wildly implausible.

Do Terrorists Deserve to Die?

Many supporters of capital punishment believe that some killers deserve to die, regardless of whether the death penalty has any specific or general deterrent effect. At least for the worst killers (and in the view of some, for all or nearly all killers), retribution alone is a sufficient basis for the death penalty. Death, in this view, is the just desert for killers.

Retributive justifications for the death penalty can also be linked to the consequences of not imposing it, which may include vigilantism. The family and friends of victims, as well as society at large, may be so outraged by a killer's crimes that they threaten to take matters into their own hands if the state does not deliver a sufficiently severe penalty.

Nonetheless, the argument for retribution does not rest on this threat. Even if there is no risk of vigilantism, retributivists argue, some killers must still be executed in the name of justice.

The retributivist argument for the death penalty is indeed strong in these cases, at least if three conditions hold. First, one must actually believe in the right of human beings to exact retribution for its own sake. Second, one must find the evidence of the defendants' guilt convincing. And third, one must be persuaded that the defendants in fact played a substantial role in the 9/11 plot. Depending on the evidence, it is possible that these conditions would hold for some but not all of the six defendants.

The Government Does Not Have to Use the Death Sentence

Importantly, to say that, based on their crimes, the defendants deserve to die, is not to say that the government is obliged to impose a death sentence. The Supreme Court's cases interpreting the Eighth Amendment's ban on cruel and unusual punishments do not directly apply of their own force to trials of aliens captured abroad and tried before military commissions. However, Section 949s of the MCA forbids "cruel and unusual punishment," and so by statute, the Court's death penalty jurisprudence may be incorporated into capital cases before military commissions. Moreover, even if the Court's Eighth Amendment precedents are not directly applicable in this way, they remain instructive in thinking about whether the government acted rightly in charging the 9/11 defendants with capital offenses.

One principle of the Court's Eighth Amendment jurisprudence, as first articulated in the 1978 case of *Lockett v. Ohio*, requires that "the sentencer, in all but the rarest kind of capital case, not be precluded from considering, as a mitigating factor, any aspect of a defendant's character or record and any of the circumstances of the offense that the defendant proffers as a basis for a sentence less than death." In a civilian murder case, this principle would be given effect by permitting a defendant to offer, for example, evidence that he was severely abused as a child or that, while in jail awaiting trial, he had sincerely repented.

The *Lockett* case does not say that the sentencing judge or jury cannot impose the death penalty on a defendant who was abused as a child, who has repented, or who has offered other evidence of mitigation. But it does require that the sentencer at least take into consideration all manner of mitigating evidence.

Still, it is very difficult to imagine that a military panel that is otherwise persuaded that the 9/11 defendants deserve to die, would impose a lesser penalty on the ground that they love their families, or grew up in poverty, or have offered any of the other sorts of evidence that are typically offered in mitigation in a civilian criminal trial.

Executing Terrorists Puts the United States at Risk

Nevertheless, there is at least one reason why the sentencing jury might conclude that a sentence of less than death is warranted: Fear of backlash. In one of his most lucid memoranda while Secretary of Defense, Donald Rumsfeld asked in 2003 whether the United States was "capturing, killing or deterring and dissuading more terrorists every day than the madrassas and the radical clerics are recruiting, training and deploying against us." The question was and remains urgent, and it is hardly obvious that executing six al Qaeda detainees after a trial that much of the world will inevitably view as unfair, will increase rather than decrease the security of the United States.

To be sure, the fact that executing Khalid Shaikh Mohammed could further fan the flames of anti-American violence is not exactly mitigating evidence, nor are Mohammed or the other defendants well-positioned to make this argument. Nonetheless, it is a valid consideration in the decision whether to charge the defendants with capital offenses. Even retributivists should care enough about consequences to settle for life imprisonment where the execution of a death sentence would likely induce the killing of more innocents.

EVALUATING THE AUTHOR'S ARGUMENTS:

Dorf argues that imposing the death penalty on convicted terrorists threatens the lives of more innocent Americans. In two or three sentences, flesh out what he means by this: How exactly would executing terrorists put more lives at risk? Then state whether you agree. Do you think executing terrorists makes the United States more or less safe? Why?

Facts About Terrorism

Editor's note: These facts can be used in reports to add credibility when making important points or claims.

Facts About Terrorist Attacks

According to 2009 National Counterterrorism Center statistics, in 2008 there were:

- 11,770 terrorist attacks worldwide;
- 8,438 attacks resulting in death, injury, or kidnapping of at least 1 person;
- 5,067 attacks resulting in the death of at least 1 individual;
- 6,703 attacks resulting in the death of no individuals;
- 2,889 attacks resulting in the death of only 1 individual;
- 235 attacks resulting in the death of at least 10 individuals;
- 4,888 attacks resulting in the injury of at least 1 individual;
- 1,125 attacks resulting in the kidnapping of at least 1 individual;
- 54,747 people killed, injured, or kidnapped as a result of terrorism;
- 15,765 people worldwide killed as a result of terrorism;
- 34,124 people worldwide injured as a result of terrorism;
- 4,858 people worldwide kidnapped as a result of terrorism.
- Compared with 2007, terrorist attacks decreased by 2,700, or 18 percent, in 2008.
- Compared with 2007, deaths due to terrorism decreased by 6,700, or 30 percent.
- The most terrorist attacks occurred in the Near East.
- The most deaths from terrorist attacks occurred in South Asia.
- The Near East and South Asia were the locations for 75 percent of the 235 high-casualty attacks (those that killed 10 or more people) in 2008.
- The number of reported attacks in 2008 fell in the Western Hemisphere by about 25 percent and in East Asia and the Pacific by 30 percent.

- The Taliban, more than any other group, claimed credit for the largest number of attacks and the highest fatality totals.
- Most 2008 attacks were perpetrated by terrorists applying conventional fighting methods such as armed attacks, bombings, and kidnappings.
- Suicide attacks declined from 525 in 2007 to 404 in 2008.
- Attacks in Iraq, Afghanistan, and Pakistan accounted for about 55 percent of all suicide attacks.
- Attacks by female suicide bombers accounted for about 9 percent of all suicide attacks worldwide and for 15 percent of all suicide attacks in Iraq.
- In 2008, more than 50 percent of the victims of terrorist attacks were Muslim; most were victims of attacks in Iraq, Pakistan, and Afghanistan.
- About 65 percent of the almost 50,000 killed or injured victims of terror were civilians.

Facts About Terrorist Plots

According to the Heritage Foundation, at least thirty planned terrorist attacks have been foiled since the September 11, 2001, attacks. These have included:
- **Richard Reid, December 2001:** Tried to ignite explosives hidden in his shoes on a flight from Paris to Miami.
- **José Padilla, May 2002:** Sentenced for planning to use a dirty bomb (an explosive laced with radioactive material) in an attack against America.
- **Lackawanna Six, September 2002:** Six men who pleaded guilty to providing support to al Qaeda.
- **Iyman Faris, May 2003:** Arrested for conspiring to use blowtorches to collapse the Brooklyn Bridge.
- **Nuradin M. Abdi, November 2003:** Pleaded guilty to conspiring to bomb a shopping mall.
- **James Elshafay and Shahawar Matin Siraj, August 2004:** Sentenced for plotting to bomb a subway station in New York City.
- **Levar Haley Washington, Gregory Vernon Patterson, Hammad Riaz Samana, and Kevin James, August 2005:** Pleaded guilty to conspiring to attack National Guard facilities, synagogues, and other targets in the Los Angeles area.

- **Michael C. Reynolds, December 2005:** Sentenced to thirty years for his involvement in a plot to blow up a Wyoming natural gas refinery; the Transcontinental Pipeline, a natural-gas pipeline from the Gulf Coast to New York and New Jersey; and a Standard Oil refinery in New Jersey.
- **Narseal Batiste, Patrick Abraham, Stanley Grant Phanor, Naudimar Herrera, Burson Augustin, Lyglenson Lemorin, and Rothschild Augustine, June 2006:** Arrested in Miami and Atlanta for plotting to blow up the Sears Tower in Chicago, FBI offices, and other government buildings.
- **Liquid Explosives Plot, August 2006:** A plot to blow up ten U.S.-bound commercial airliners with liquid explosives, foiled by British law enforcement.
- **Derrick Shareef, December 2006:** Sentenced for planning to set off hand grenades in a Chicago-area shopping mall.
- **Fort Dix Plot, May 2007:** Five of six men found guilty for plotting to attack Fort Dix, a U.S. Army post in New Jersey.
- **Airport Plot, June 2007:** Four men charged with plotting to blow up fuel tanks and pipelines at the John F. Kennedy International Airport in New York City.
- **Hosam Maher Husein Smadi, September 2009:** Charged for his involvement in a plot to bomb a Dallas skyscraper.
- **Michael Finton, September 2009:** Arrested after trying to detonate a car bomb outside a federal building in Springfield, Illinois.
- **Umar Farouk Abdulmutallab, the Christmas Day Bomber, 2009:** Arrested for trying to ignite a bomb hidden in his underwear on a flight from Amsterdam to Detroit.
- **Raja Lahrasib Khan, March 2010:** Arrested for providing material support to a foreign terrorist organization.
- **Times Square Attempted Car Bombing, May 2010:** A car bomb left in New York City's Time Square fails to explode.

American Opinions About Terrorism

According to a 2010 CNN/Opinion Research Corporation poll:
- Sixty percent of Americans think the United States should continue to operate the terrorist detention facility in Guantánamo Bay, Cuba;

- 39 percent think the facility should be closed.
- Fifty-five percent of Americans think it is extremely important for the president and Congress to deal with the issue of terrorism in the upcoming year;
- 33 percent think it is very important;
- 9 percent think it is moderately important;
- 2 percent think it is not that important.

According to a 2010 Ipsos/McClatchy poll:
- Fifty-one percent of Americans think it is necessary to give up some civil liberties in order to make the country safe from terrorism;
- 36 percent think some of the government's antiterrorism proposals will go too far in restricting the public's civil liberties;
- 8 percent said it depends;
- 5 percent were unsure.
- Eighty-two percent of Americans think better coordination of intelligence collected by different government agencies about potentially dangerous passengers can reduce the risk of terrorism;
- 74 percent think body scans or full-body searches at airports can reduce the risk of terrorism;
- 57 percent think restrictions on carry-on luggage can reduce the risk of terrorism;
- 49 percent think restrictions on in-flight activity, such as banning the use of electronic equipment, requiring passengers to stay seated or to keep any item off their laps, can reduce the risk of terrorism.

According to a 2010 *USA Today*/Gallup poll:
- Fifty-three percent of Americans think the U.S. government has made a "fair amount" of progress in protecting the country from terrorism since 9/11;
- 22 percent think the U.S. government has made "not much" progress;
- 21 percent think the U.S. government has made "a great deal" of progress;
- 4 percent think no progress has been made at all.

- Seventy-one percent of Americans think airline passengers who fit the profile of terrorists based on their age, ethnicity, or gender should be subjected to special, more intensive security checks before boarding U.S. flights;
- 27 percent oppose the profiling of airline passengers;
- 2 percent are unsure.

According to a 2010 CBS News poll:
- Seven percent of Americans give the United States an "A" for its ability to protect the country from a terrorist attack;
- 28 percent of Americans give the United States a "B" for its ability to protect the country from a terrorist attack;
- 42 percent of Americans give the United States a "C" for its ability to protect the country from a terrorist attack;
- 14 percent of Americans give the United States a "D" for its ability to protect the country from a terrorist attack;
- 6 percent of Americans give the United States an "F" for its ability to protect the country from a terrorist attack.

Forty percent of Americans think it is somewhat likely there will be another terrorist attack in the United States within the next few months;
- 26 percent think it is very likely;
- 22 percent think it is not very likely;
- 8 percent think it is not likely at all;
- 4 percent are unsure.

Glossary

anthrax: A deadly bacterium used in the October 2001 bioterrorism attacks that killed five people.

Aum Shinrikyo: Japanese cult that released sarin nerve gas in the Tokyo subway system in 1995. Twelve people were killed.

bioterrorism: Terrorism that involves the intentional release of a deadly or toxic bacterium or virus.

dirty bomb: Also called a radiological dispersal device (RDD), a crudely built radioactive bomb that spreads radioactive material over an area, sickening and killing those who are exposed.

FARC (Revolutionary Armed Forces of Colombia): Colombia's oldest and largest insurgent group.

Hamas: Palestinian group whose mission is to oust Israel from the West Bank and the Gaza Strip. Responsible for multiple terrorist attacks on Israeli military and civilian entities. Hamas operates a political and a humanitarian wing.

Hizbollah: Anti-Israel Palestinian group based in Lebanon. Receives funding and support from Iran.

jihad: An Arabic term that literally means "struggle." Has been interpreted by some to mean "holy war" and used by Islamo-terrorists to justify terrorist attacks against the West.

9/11 Commission: The independent bipartisan group tasked with preparing a full and complete account of the circumstances surrounding the September 11, 2001, terrorist attacks.

al Qaeda: Osama bin Laden's terrorist group responsible for carrying out numerous acts of terrorism, including the September 11, 2001, terrorist attacks.

sarin gas: Toxic nerve gas. One of the most likely toxic chemicals to be used in a chemical terrorist attack.

smallpox: Deadly virus that experts fear could be released in a bioterrorist attack.

state-sponsored terrorism: Acts of terrorism carried out with help from a national government. The U.S. State Department considers Cuba, Iran, North Korea, the Sudan, and Syria to be state sponsors of terrorism.

Taliban: The former leaders of Afghanistan who granted Osama bin Laden safe haven after the 9/11 attacks. Taliban forces continue to fight U.S. and coalition soldiers in Afghanistan and have set up insurgency groups in other nations, such as Pakistan.

weapons of mass destruction (WMDs): Nuclear, biological, chemical, and radiological weapons capable of enormous destruction, death, and injury.

Organizations to Contact

The editors have compiled the following list of organizations concerned with the issues debated in this book. The descriptions are derived from materials provided by the organizations. All have publications or information available for interested readers. The list was compiled on the date of publication of the present volume; the information provided here may change. Be aware that many organizations take several weeks or longer to respond to inquiries, so allow as much time as possible for the receipt of requested materials.

American Civil Liberties Union (ACLU)
125 Broad St., 18th Floor
New York, NY 10004-2400
(212) 549-2500
e-mail: aclu@aclu.org
Web site: www.aclu.org

The American Civil Liberties Union works to defend Americans' civil rights guaranteed by the U.S. Constitution. It argues in courts, legislatures, and communities to preserve individual liberties, such as freedom of speech, freedom of the press, and privacy rights. Following the September 2001 terrorist attacks, the ACLU founded its National Security Project, which litigates national security cases involving discrimination, torture, detention, surveillance, and secrecy, to protect every human's fundamental rights.

Center for Defense Information (CDI)
1779 Massachusetts Ave. NW, Ste. 615
Washington, DC 20036
(202) 332-0600
fax: (202) 462-4559
e-mail: info@cdi.org
Web site: www.cdi.org

The Center for Defense Information is a nonpartisan, nonprofit organization that researches all aspects of global security. It seeks to educate the public and policy makers about issues such as nuclear weapons, security policy, and terrorist threats through its numerous programs, including Homeland Defense, Terrorism, and Nuclear Proliferation, to name a few.

Center for Nonproliferation Studies
460 Pierce St.
Monterey, CA 93940
(831) 647-4154
fax: (831) 647-3519
e-mail: cns@miis.edu
Web site: http://cns.miis.edu

The center researches all aspects of nonproliferation and works to combat weapons of mass destruction falling into terrorist hands. The center produces research databases and has multiple reports, papers, speeches, and congressional testimony available online. Its main publication is the *Nonproliferation Review*, which is published three times per year.

Center for Strategic and International Studies (CSIS)
1800 K St. NW
Washington, DC 20006
(202) 887-0200
fax: (202) 775-3199
e-mail: webmaster@csis.org
Web site: www.csis.org

CSIS is a bipartisan public policy think tank that focuses on America's economic policy, national security, and foreign and domestic policies. The center conducts research and provides strategic insight and policy solutions for government decision makers. It produces ample reports about national security and terrorism.

Council on American-Muslim Relations (CAIR)
453 New Jersey Ave. SE
Washington, DC 20003
(202) 488-8787
fax: (202) 488-0833

e-mail: cair@cair-net.org
Web site: www.cair-net.org

CAIR is a nonprofit organization that works to defend the rights of American Muslims. It offers an Islamic perspective on public policy issues. The CAIR Web site features statements condemning the September 11, 2001, terrorist attacks and documents subsequent discrimination against Muslims.

Department of Homeland Security (DHS)
Washington, DC 20528
(202) 282-8000
Web site: www.dhs.gov

The Department of Homeland Security was created after the September 11, 2001, terrorist attacks. The department serves to secure the nation while preserving American freedoms and liberties. It is charged with protecting the United States from terrorists, decreasing the country's vulnerability to terrorism, and effectively responding to attacks. The current DHS homeland security strategic plan can be found on its Web site.

Federal Aviation Administration (FAA)
800 Independence Ave. SW
Washington, DC 20591
(866) 835-5322
fax: (202) 267-3484
Web site: www.faa.gov

The Federal Aviation Administration is an agency of the U.S. Department of Transportation whose primary responsibility is to maintain civil aviation safety standards. The FAA's major functions include regulating civil aviation to promote safety and fulfill the requirements of national defense.

Federal Bureau of Investigation
935 Pennsylvania Ave. NW
Washington, DC 20535-0001
(202) 324-3000
Web site: www.fbi.gov

The FBI works hand in hand with law enforcement agencies, intelligence organizations, the military, and diplomatic circles to neutralize terrorist cells and operatives in the United States and to dismantle terrorist networks worldwide.

Federation of American Scientists
1717 K St. NW, Ste. 209
Washington, DC 20036
(202) 546-3300
Web site: www.fas.org

The Federation of American Scientists was formed in 1945 by atomic scientists from the Manhattan Project who felt that scientists, engineers, and other innovators had an ethical obligation to bring their knowledge and experience to bear on critical national decisions, especially pertaining to the technology they had unleashed—the atomic bomb. The FAS publishes reports on many issues of national and political significance, including counterterrorism and the threat of a biological, chemical, or nuclear attack.

Global Exchange
2017 Mission St. #303
San Francisco, CA 94110
(415) 255-7296
fax: (415) 255-7498
Web site: www.globalexchange.org

Global Exchange is a human rights organization that seeks to solve global injustice through education, activism, and a noninterventionist U.S. foreign policy. Global Exchange opposes military retaliation to terrorist attacks.

Henry L. Stimson Center
1111 Nineteenth St. NW, 12th Floor
Washington, DC 20036
(202) 223-5956
e-mail: info@stimson.org
Web site: www.stimson.org

The Stimson Center is an independent, nonprofit public policy institute committed to finding and promoting innovative solutions to the security challenges confronting the United States and other nations. The center directs the Chemical and Biological Weapons Nonproliferation Project, which serves as a clearinghouse of information related to the monitoring and implementation of the 1993 Chemical Weapons Convention.

Institute for Policy Studies (IPS)
1112 Sixteenth St. NW, Ste. 600
Washington, DC 20036
(202) 234-9382
fax: (202) 387-7915
e-mail: info@ips-dc.org
Web site: www. ips-dc.org

The Institute for Policy Studies is a nonprofit think tank dedicated to progressive or liberal causes. Founded in 1963, IPS was created to provide independent research and education to address public policy problems in Washington. Its numerous projects are all dedicated to pursuing peace, justice, and a healthy environment. Numerous national security reports and papers can be found on its Web site.

International Policy Institute for Counter-Terrorism (ICT)
PO Box 167
Herzlia, 46150, Israel
972-9-9527277
fax: 972-9-9513073
e-mail: info@ict.org.il
Web site: www.ict.org.il

This research institute develops public policy solutions to international terrorism. Its Web site is a comprehensive resource on terrorism and counterterrorism, including an extensive database on terrorist organizations.

National Counterterrorism Center (NCTC)
Web site: www.nctc.gov

The National Counterterrorism Center is charged with analyzing terrorism intelligence, storing terrorism information, and providing lists of terrorists, terrorist groups, and worldwide terrorist incidents to the intelligence community. The NCTC also writes assessments and briefings for policy makers. The NCTC's online Press Room contains press releases, interviews, speeches and testimony, fact sheets, and published reports, as well as the legislation that guides the center's actions.

National Security Agency (NSA)
9800 Savage Rd.
Ft. George Meade, MD 20755
(301) 688-6524
fax: (301) 688-6198
Web site: www.nsa.gov

The NSA is a cryptologic agency administered by the U.S. Department of Defense. Its main goal is to protect national security systems and to produce foreign intelligence information. The NSA follows U.S. laws to defeat terrorist organizations at home and abroad and ensures the protection of privacy and civil liberties of American citizens. Speeches, congressional testimonies, press releases, and research reports are all available on the NSA Web site.

Transportation Security Administration (TSA)
601 S. Twelfth St.
Arlington, VA 20598
(866) 289-9673
e-mail: tsa-contactcenter@dhs.gov
Web site: www.tsa.gov

The Transportation Security Administration was created in 2001 following the September 11 terrorist attacks and is an agency that serves the U.S. Department of Homeland Security. It is responsible for security in all modes of transportation, including highways, railroads, buses, mass transit systems, ports and 450 U.S. airports, but particularly aviation security. The TSA also has a number of airline security programs, including the Alien Flight Student Program and the Certified Cargo Screening Program, to ensure the safety of the entire airline industry.

For Further Reading

Books

Berman, Eli. *Radical, Religious, and Violent: The New Economics of Terrorism.* Cambridge, MA: MIT Press, 2009. Argues that radical religious terrorists are not generally motivated by the promise of rewards in the afterlife or even by religious ideas in general. Instead, these terrorists are best understood as rational altruists seeking to help their own communities.

Burleigh, Michael. *Blood and Rage: A Cultural History of Terrorism.* New York: HarperPerennial, 2010. Traces modern terrorism's roots to the mid-nineteenth century and argues that terrorism is a career, a culture, and a way of life attractive for its own sake as well as its ostensible objectives.

Burton, Fred. *Ghost: Confessions of a Counterterrorism Agent.* New York: Random House, 2009. A former counterterrorism agent shares what counterterrorism really means on a day-to-day level.

Combs, Cynthia C. *Terrorism in the Twenty-First Century.* Englewood Cliffs, NJ: Prentice-Hall, 2010. Puts terrorism into historical perspective and analyzes it as a form of political violence. Presents the most essential concepts, the latest data, and numerous case studies to promote effective analysis of terrorist acts.

Cronin, Audrey Kurth. *How Terrorism Ends: Understanding the Decline and Demise of Terrorist Campaigns.* Princeton, NJ: Princeton University Press, 2009. Examines how terrorist campaigns have met their demise over the past two centuries and applies these enduring lessons to outline a new strategy against al Qaeda.

Kobrin, Nancy Hartevelt. *The Banality of Suicide Terrorism: The Naked Truth About the Psychology of Islamic Suicide Bombing.* Dulles, VA: Potomac, 2010. Dismantles the psychological dynamics of suicide terrorism.

Krueger, Alan B. *What Makes a Terrorist: Economics and the Roots of Terrorism.* Princeton, NJ: Princeton University Press, 2008. Argues against the notion that terrorism can be defeated through aid and education. Contends that an aggressive foreign policy based on this erroneous assumption has cost several nations dearly and continuing along this course may provoke further terrorist acts.

Mueller, John. *Overblown: How Politicians and the Terrorism Industry Inflate National Security Threats, and Why We Believe Them.* New York: Free Press, 2009. Argues that terrorism hypervigilance is threatening civil liberties, the economy, and lives.

Napoleoni, Loretta. *Terrorism and the Economy: How the War on Terror Is Bankrupting the World.* New York: Seven Stories, 2010. Traces the link between the finances of the war on terror and the global economic crisis. Argues that if the United States does not face up to the many serious connections between its response to 9/11 and the financial crisis, it will never work its way out of the looming global recession that now threatens Americans' way of life.

Pape, Robert. *Dying to Win: The Strategic Logic of Suicide Terrorism.* New York: Random House, 2006. Offers a groundbreaking profile of suicide terrorist attackers. Finds that, contrary to conventional wisdom, the group responsible for the most suicide attacks is not religious in nature.

Post, Jerrold M. *The Mind of the Terrorist: The Psychology of Terrorism from the IRA to al-Qaeda.* New York: Palgrave Macmillan, 2008. Identifies and explores three types of terrorism: national-separatist, social-revolutionary, and religious-extremist. Argues that understanding the psychology and sociology of terrorists is vital in a true war on terrorism.

Sheehan, Michael A. *Crush the Cell: How to Defeat Terrorism Without Terrorizing Ourselves.* New York: Three Rivers, 2009. Argues that the United States has wasted billions of dollars on the wrong kinds of protective measures in the war on terror. Examines the mystery surrounding terrorist cells and argues that "terror experts" and members of the media are playing into the terrorists' hands.

Simonsen, Clifford E., and Jeremy R. Spindlove. *Terrorism Today: The Past, the Players, the Future.* 4th ed. Englewood Cliffs, NJ: Prentice-Hall, 2009. Offers an evaluation of the enduring role of terrorism on the world stage. Addresses the past, significant players, and future implications of a struggle that threatens the world's safety and security.

Thiessen, Marc A. *Courting Disaster: How the CIA Kept America Safe and How Barack Obama Is Inviting the Next Attack*. Washington, DC: Regnery, 2010. A former White House speechwriter explains how the CIA's interrogation program begun under President George W. Bush—shut down by President Barack Obama—thwarted specific deadly attacks against the United States.

Tripathi, Deepak. *Breeding Ground: Afghanistan and the Origins of Islamist Terrorism*. Dulles, VA: Potomac, 2010. Explains how Afghanistan descended into a civil war that produced the Taliban. Calls for U.S. officials to replace their military strategy with an approach that is centered on development, internal reconciliation, and societal reconstruction in Afghanistan.

White, Jonathan R. *Terrorism and Homeland Security: An Introduction*. Florence, KY: Wadsworth, 2008. Offers specific examples that enable readers to understand how terrorism arises and how it functions. Discusses essential historical background on the phenomenon of terrorism and the roots of contemporary conflicts and includes detailed descriptions of recent and contemporary conflicts shaping the world stage.

Periodicals

Allison, Graham. "Preventing a Nuclear Terrorist Attack," *Washington Times*, March 30, 2008. www.washingtontimes.com/news/2008/mar/30/preventing-a-nuclear-terrorist-attack.

Baker, Rodger. "Ricin: An Unlikely Weapon of Mass Destruction," STRATFOR, March 5, 2008. www.stratfor.com/weekly/ricin_unlikely_weapon_mass_destruction.

Bergen, Peter. "The Terrorists Among Us: Why an al Qaeda Attack on U.S. Soil Is Still a Real Threat," *Foreign Policy in Focus,* November 19, 2009. www.foreignpolicy.com/articles/2009/11/18/the_terrorists_among_us?page=0,0.

Bergen, Peter. "WMD Terrorism Is Overblown," CNN.com, December 5, 2008. www.cnn.com/2008/POLITICS/12/05/bergen.wmd.

Boteach, Shmuley. "The Death Penalty for Terrorists," *Jerusalem Post*, July 21, 2008. www.jpost.com/servlet/Satellite?cid=l2153310470 48&pagename=JPArticle%2FShowFull.

Bunn, Matthew. "Thwarting Terrorists: More to Be Done," *Washington Post*, September 26, 2007. www.washingtonpost.com/ wp-dyn/content/article/2007/09/25/AR2007092501347.html.

Emery, Aaron. "Water Boarding and the Future State of Torture," Campaign for Liberty, July 3, 2009. www.campaignforliberty.com/ article.php?view=110.

Etzioni, Amitai. "Deproliferation: An Approach to Preventing Nuclear Terrorism," *Bulletin of the Atomic Scientists*, July 23, 2008. www.thebulletin.org/web-edition/opeds/deproliferation-approach-to-preventing-nuclear-terrorism.

Flynn, Stephen. "America Remains at Risk—from Itself," *Newsweek*, December 7, 2009. www.newsweek.com/id/225632.

Gardham, Duncan. "Is the 'War on Terrorism' Better Fought at Home?" *Daily Telegraph* (London), November 9, 2009. www .telegraph.co.uk/news/uknews/6531501/Is-the-war-on-terrorism-better-fought-at-home.html.

Gerson, Michael. "On Holding the Terrorist Trials: Attorney General Is Making Grave Mistake," *San Francisco Chronicle*, November 18, 2009. www.sfgate.com/cgi-bin/article.cgi?f=/c/a/2009/11/17/ ED9K1ALUS8.DTL#ixzz0Z2xIrpR3.

Goldberg, Jonah. "It's No Way to Fight a War on Terror," *National Review*, November 18, 2009. http://article.nationalreview.com/?q =ZGV1ODV1ZDEzZTc5NWI4NzMwNDMxMDU3NjE5NG EjMjU=&w=MA==.

Greenberg, Karen J. "8 Reasons to Close Guantanamo Now," *In These Times*, February 12, 2007. www.inthesetimes.com/article/3024.

Hansen, Jonathan. "Don't Close Gitmo," *Guardian* (Manchester), June 2, 2009. www.guardian.co.uk/commentisfree/cifamerica/ 2009/may/28/guantanamo-obama-truth-and-reconciliation.

Krauthammer, Charles. "Travesty in New York," *Washington Post*, November 20, 2009. www.washingtonpost.com/wp-dyn/content/ article/2009/11/19/AR2009111903434.html?nav=rss-opinion/ columns.

Lawson, Guy. "The Fear Factory," *Rolling Stone*, February 7, 2008. www.rollingstone.com/politics/story/18137343/the_fear_factory.

Lind, Michael. "How I Learned to Stop Worrying and Live with the Bomb," *Salon*, October 13, 2009. www.salon.com/opinion/feature/2009/l0/13/nuclear_weapons.

McCarthy, Andrew C. "Why Close Gitmo? Its Critics Will Never Be Satisfied," *National Review*, February 25, 2009. http://article.nationalreview.com/?q=N2E1NGJiMjZhOGY2YzExZjYwMWM1MTA3YmZhNzFlNiU=.

McNamara, Sally. "Why NATO Must Win in Afghanistan: A Central Front in the War on Terrorism," *Backgrounder* #2148, Heritage Foundation, June 23, 2008. www.heritage.org/research/Europe/bg2148.cfm.

Montgomery, Evan Braden. *Nuclear Terrorism: Assessing the Threat, Developing a Response*, Center for Strategic and Budgetary Assessments, 2009. www.csbaonline.org/4Publications/PubLibrary/R.20090422.Nuclear_Terrorism/R.20090422.Nuclear_Terrorism.pdf.

Mueller, John. "The 'Safe Haven' Myth," *Nation*, October 21, 2009. www.thenation.com/doc/20091109/nmeller/print.

New York Daily News. "Enemies Within: America Must Face the Threat Posed by Homegrown Terrorists," September 26, 2009. www.nydailynews.com/opinions/2009/09/26/2009-09-26_enemies_within_america_must_face_the_threat_posed_by_home grown_terrorists.html#ixzz0Z2Qn6Art.

Robinson, Eugene. "A Battlefield in the Courtroom," *Washington Post*, November 20, 2009. www.washingtonpost.com/wp-dyn/content/article/2009/11/19/AR2009111903433.html?nav=rss_opinion/columns.

Shultz, George P., William J. Perry, Henry A. Kissinger, and Sam Nunn. "A World Free of Nuclear Weapons," *Washington Post*, January 4, 2007. www.nuclearsecurityproiect.org/atf/cf/%7B1fce2821-c31c-4560-becl-bb4bb58b54d9%7D/A-WORLD-FREE-OF-NUCLEAR-WEAPONS.PDF.

STRATFOR. "Debunking Myths About Nuclear Weapons and Terrorism," May 29, 2009. www.stratfor.com/analysis/20090528_debunking_myths_about_nuclear_weapons_and_terrorism.

Third Way. "Keeping Nuclear Weapons Out of the Hands of Terrorists," National Security Program #5, September 2008. www.thirdway.org/data/product/file/165/NS_Mod5_Keeping_Nuclear_Weapons_from_Terrorists.pdf.

Vartabedian, Ralph. "How the U.S. Seeks to Avert Nuclear Terrorism," *Los Angeles Times*, January 6, 2008. http://articles.latimes.com/2008/jan/06/nation/na-nuke6.

Walt, Stephen M. "The Afpak Muddle (Part 2): How Serious Is the Threat?" *Foreign Policy in Focus*, April 6, 2009. http://walt.foreignpolicy.com/posts/2009/04/06/the_afpak_muddle_part_2_how_serious_is_the_threat.

Winship, Michael. "New York Is Tough Enough for Terrorist Trials," Common Dreams.org, November 21, 2009. www.commondreams.org/view/2009/11/21-7.

Web Sites

The Counter-Terrorism Page (www.terrorism.net). Offers objective breaking news on terrorism-related issues from a variety of sources including governments, nongovernmental organizations, academics, and professionals.

Country Reports on Terrorism (www.state.gov/s/ct/rls/crt). This site offers free downloadable PDFs of current and previous State Department reports on terrorism. An invaluable source of terrorism-related statistics and facts for student reports.

Global Terrorism Database (www.start.umd.edu/gtd). This database offers information on terrorist events around the world from 1970 through the present. Unlike other event databases, the GTD includes systematic data on domestic as well as international terrorist incidents that have occurred during this time period and now includes more than eighty thousand cases.

The Investigative Project on Terrorism (www.investigativeproject.org). The IPT investigates the operations, funding, activities, and front groups of Islamic terrorist and extremist groups in the United States and around the world. Research carried out by the IPT team has formed the basis for thousands of articles and television specials on the subject of radical Islamic involvement in terrorism, and it has even led to successful government action against terrorists and financiers based in the United States.

RAND Database of Worldwide Terrorism Incidents (RDWTI) (www.rand.org/nsrd/projects/terrorism-incidents). A searchable database of terrorist incidents dating back to 1972. Incidents are searchable by date, target, weapon, perpetrator, and more.

The Terrorism Awareness Project (www.terrorismawareness.org). In addition to news and information, the Terrorism Awareness Project publishes videos by terrorist groups to demonstrate the extent to which terrorist groups are dangerous and radical.

Terrorism Files (www.terrorismfiles.org). A clearinghouse of daily breaking news articles related to terrorism.

Terrorist Designation Lists (www.state.gov/s/ct/list). This site, run by the U.S. State Department, offers lists of known terrorists groups both foreign and domestic.

Index

Picture Credits

AP Images, 11, 15, 35, 41, 46, 50, 62, 81, 88, 100, 110, 127

Ahmed Jadallah/Reuters/Landov, 23

Kevin Lamarque/Reuters/Landov, 117

Landov, 53

John Milli/GPO via Getty Images, 132

Reuters/Middle East Broadcasting/Landov, 8

Mike Segar/Reuters/Landov, 95

Jim Young/Reuters/Landov, 105

Steve Zmina, 16, 20, 28, 54, 61, 71, 76, 83, 106, 119, 124, 137